# Books by Dr. John C. Maxwell
# Can Teach You How to Be a REAL Success

## Relationships

*25 Ways to Win with People*

*Becoming a Person of Influence*

*Encouragement Changes Everything*

*Ethics 101*

*Everyone Communicates, Few Connect*

*The Power of Partnership*

*Relationships 101*

*Winning with People*

## Equipping

*The 15 Invaluable Laws of Growth*

*The 17 Essential Qualities
of a Team Player*

*The 17 Indisputable Laws of Teamwork*

*Developing the Leaders Around You*

*How Successful People Grow*

*Equipping 101*

*JumpStart Your Growth*

*Learning from the Giants*

*Make Today Count*

*Mentoring 101*

*My Dream Map*

*The 21 Most Powerful Minutes in a Leader's Day*

*The 360 Degree Leader*

*Developing the Leader Within You*

*JumpStart Your Leadership*

*Good Leaders Ask Great Questions*

*The 5 Levels of Leadership*

*Go for Gold*

*How Successful People Lead*

*Leadership 101*

*Leadership Gold*

*Leadership Promises for Every Day*

# INTENTIONAL LIVING

## CHOOSING A LIFE THAT MATTERS

## JOHN C. MAXWELL

CENTER STREET

LARGE PRINT

The author is represented by Yates & Yates, www.yates2.com.

Center Street
Hachette Book Group
1290 Avenue of the Americas
New York, NY 10104

www.CenterStreet.com

Printed in the United States of America

RRD-H

First edition: October 2015

10 9 8 7 6 5 4 3 2 1

Center Street is a division of Hachette Book Group, Inc.
The Center Street name and logo are trademarks of
Hachette Book Group, Inc.

The Hachette Speakers Bureau provides a wide range of authors
for speaking events. To find out more, go to
www.HachetteSpeakersBureau.com or call (866) 376-6591.

The publisher is not responsible for websites (or their content) that are not
owned by the publisher.

Library of Congress Cataloging-in-Publication Data
has been applied for.

ISBN: 978-1-4555-3621-4 (large print)

*This book is dedicated to Chris Hodges. Thank you, Chris, for the many conversations we've had about how to live an intentional life.*

*Your words have given me insight.*

*Your life has backed up those words.*

*Your friendship has been a well of water I have often drunk from.*

*No one lives an intentional life better than you do.*

# Contents

# Acknowledgments

Thank you to:

Laura Morton, who sat with me for hours asking me questions and helping me remember my story

Stephanie Wetzel, my social media manager, who helped with the book's structure and research

Charlie Wetzel, my longtime writer who crafted and polished the manuscript

Linda Eggers, my executive assistant who helps me to remain intentional every day

# 1

## Your Life Can Be a Great Story

What's your life story?

When I meet people for the first time, as soon as the introductions are out of the way, I ask them to share their stories—to tell me who they are and where they're from, where they've been and where they're going. I want to understand what matters to them. Maybe you do the same. The telling of our stories becomes an emotional connecting point for us. It bridges the gap between us.

Why is that?

Everyone loves a good story—we always have. Stories tell us who we are. They...

- Inspire us.
- Connect with us.
- Animate our reasoning process.

- Give us permission to act.
- Fire our emotions.
- Give us pictures of who we aspire to be.

Stories *are* us.

Every day millions of people watch movies, read novels, and search the Internet for stories that inspire them or make them laugh. Every day we listen to our friends tell us about the dramatic or funny things that happen to them. Every day people take out their smartphones to show pictures and share stories. Stories are how we relate to others, learn, and remember.

As a communicator, I spend a good portion of my days sharing stories. People don't care a lot about cold facts. They don't want to look at pie charts. They want excitement. They like drama. They care about pictures. They want to laugh. They want to see and feel what happened. Statistics don't inspire people to do great things. Stories do!

## What's Your Story?

So I'll ask you again: What's your story?

I wish I could sit with you right now and hear it from you. When you get to the end of this book, I'll tell you about a way you *can* share your story with me and with others. But before we get to that, I want you to think about your story so far. What kind of story is it?

We all have a bit of humor in our stories, as well as some drama. We all have our ups and downs, wins and losses. There's a bit of comedy, tragedy, and history in all of us. But overall, each of our lives tells a larger story. What do you want yours to say?

I believe that no matter what "plot" each of our stories may follow, deep down we all want one thing. **We want our lives to matter. We want our stories to be of significance.** Nobody wants to feel like the world wouldn't miss him if he'd never lived. Are you with me?

Have you ever seen the classic movie *It's a Wonderful Life*? It's the story of George Bailey, a man who dreams of traveling the world and building things, but who instead stays home in Bedford Falls, because he repeatedly chooses to do what he believes to be right for others. A point occurs in the movie where George experiences a moment of crisis, and he comes to believe that everyone around him would be better off if he had never been born. What he's really saying is that his life doesn't matter.

The great twist in the story occurs when, with the help of an angel, George gets a chance to see what his town and others' lives would look like if he had never existed. Without him, it's a dark and negative place. George comes to recognize the positive impact he had made because, time after time, he took action to do what he knew was right and helped other people. As Clarence the angel tells him, "Each man's life touches so many other lives." George had touched many lives in small ways and made a difference.

Have you looked at your life from that angle? Have you thought about what you want your life story to be? Do you believe you can live a life of significance, that you can do things that really matter? Can you make your story great?

With all my heart, I believe the answer to these questions is yes. You have it within your power to make your life a great story, one of significance. Every person can. Regardless of nationality, opportunity, ethnicity, or capacity, each of us can live a life of significance. We can do things that matter and that can make the world a better place. I hope you believe that. If you don't now, I hope you will by the time you're finished reading this book.

Don't let the word *significance* intimidate you. Don't let it stop you from pursuing a life that matters. When I talk about significance, I'm not talking about being famous. I'm not talking about getting rich. I'm not talking about being a huge celebrity or winning a Nobel Prize or becoming the president of the United

States. There's nothing wrong with any of those things, but you don't have to accomplish any of them to be significant. To be significant, all you have to do is make a difference with others wherever you are, with whatever you have, day by day.

> To be significant, all you have to do is make a difference with others wherever you are, with whatever you have, day by day.

Back in 1976, I received a gift from Eileen Beavers, who was my assistant at that time. As I unwrapped it, I saw it was a book, and I was intrigued by the title: *The Greatest Story Ever Told.* I couldn't wait to read it.

But when I opened it, I was shocked. The pages were blank.

Inside was a note from Eileen that said, "John, your life is before you. Fill these pages with kind acts, good thoughts, and matters of your heart. Write a great story with your life."

I still remember the excitement and anticipation that surged through me when I read her words. For the first time it made me think about how I was the author of my life, and I could fill every "page" with whatever I wanted. It made me want to be significant. It inspired me to do whatever I could to make my life matter.

So what's the secret to filling the pages of your life? What's the key to a life that matters?

*Living each day with intentionality.*

When you live each day with intentionality, there's almost no limit to what you can do. You can trans-form yourself, your family, your community, and your nation. When enough people do that, they can change the world. When you intention-ally use your everyday life to bring about positive change in the lives of others, you begin to live a life that matters.

> When you intentionally use your everyday life to bring about positive change in the lives of others, you begin to live a life that matters.

I vividly remember watching Reese Witherspoon's emotional acceptance speech after she won the Best Actress Academy Award in 2006 for portraying June Carter Cash in *Walk the Line.* Witherspoon said that people often asked June how she was doing, and she'd say, "I'm just tryin' to matter!" The actress went on to say that she understood exactly what June meant because she too was trying to make her life matter— by living a good life and doing work that meant something to somebody.

And isn't that what all of us want? To make our lives matter? So if that is true, why doesn't it happen for everybody?

## Get into the Story

Most people want to hear or tell a good story. But they don't realize they can and should *be* the good story. That requires intentional living. It is the bridge that crosses the gap to a life that matters. I'll explain this in detail in the next chapter, but right now I'll just say this: when unintentional people see the wrongs of the world, they say, "Something should be done about that." They see or hear a story, and they react to it emotionally and intellectually. But they go no further.

People who live intentionally jump in and live the story themselves. The words of physicist Albert Einstein motivate them: "The world is a dangerous place, not because of those who do evil, but because of those who look on and do nothing."

Why do so many people do nothing? I think it's because most of us look at the evils and injustice around us, and we become overwhelmed. The problems look too big for us to tackle. We say to ourselves, "What can I do? I'm just one person."

One person is a start. One person can act and make a change by helping another. One person can inspire a second person to be intentional, and another. Those people can work together. They can become a movement. They can make an impact. We should never let what we *cannot* do keep us from doing what we *can* do. A passive life does not become a meaningful life.

Not long ago I read *A Million Miles in a Thousand Years* by Don Miller. He eloquently writes about seeing our lives as stories. He explains, "I've never walked out of a meaningless movie thinking all movies are meaningless. I only thought the movie I walked out on was meaningless. I wonder, then, if when people say life is meaningless, what they really mean is *their* lives are meaningless. I wonder if they've chosen to believe their whole existence is unremarkable, and are projecting their dreary lives on the rest of us."[1]

If you are reading these words and thinking to yourself, *That's me. My life is meaningless. My existence is unremarkable. I wish my life were less dreary,* then I have good news for you. This doesn't have to be your story. Your story can be about a life that matters.

Don Miller also writes, "You can call it God or a conscience, or you can dismiss it as that intuitive knowing we all have as human beings, as living storytellers; but there is a knowing I feel that guides me toward better stories, toward being a better character. I believe there is a writer outside ourselves, plotting a better story for us, interacting with us, even, and whispering a better story into our consciousness."[2]

No matter what your beliefs are, I can tell you this. If your story isn't as meaningful or significant or compelling as you want it to be, you can change it. You can begin writing a new story, beginning today. Don't settle for being merely a teller of stories about significance. Decide to *be* the story of significance. Become the central character in your story of making a difference!

> If your story isn't as meaningful or significant or compelling as you want it to be, you can change it.

## Your Story, Not History

I have to admit, this notion goes against everything I learned in college. It may go against your education, too. In the courses I took on speaking, the professors taught us to take our stories from history, not to draw upon personal experiences to illustrate our points. They believed to do anything other than that appeared egocentric.

As a bourgeoning communicator, however, I observed that the greatest speakers didn't just tell better stories. They actually made the stories better by living them first. Their stories came from their experiences. They were at the heart of their best stories.

And that's what I want for you. I don't want you to be merely a *storyteller* of significance. I want you to be a *story liver*! Your story still has many blank pages. You can write on them with your life. When you get right down to it, intentional living is about living your best story.

One of the biggest comedy acts of the sixties and seventies was the Smothers Brothers. I remember a routine they performed on their television variety show that went something like this:

"What's wrong, Tommy?" asked Dick, who was the straight man. "You seem a bit despondent."

"I am!" replied his brother Tommy. "I'm worried about the state of our American society!"

"Well, what bothers you about it? Are you worried about the extent of poverty and hunger in the land?"

"Oh no, that doesn't really bother me."

"I see. Well, are you concerned about the growing threat of nuclear war?"

"No, that's not a worry of mine."

"Are you upset about the use and abuse of drugs by the youth of America?"

"No, that doesn't bother me very much."

Looking rather puzzled, Dick asked, "Well, Tom, if you're not bothered by poverty and hunger, war and drugs, what are you worried about?"

"I'm worried about our apathy!"

Apathetic people will never make their world different. Indifferent people will not live a life that matters. Passive people take themselves out of the greatest of all stories—their own. Maybe they want to see themselves in the story, but they exist as mere observers on the sidelines. They wish for more, but they fail to become active participants. Why? Because they are unintentional.

## How to Start Writing Your Significance Story

If you're like me and want to make a difference and have a significance story to tell by the end of your life, I can help you. I'm going to show you the simple pathway toward intentional living. But first, you need to be willing to take an important step forward. And that comes from a change in mindset, from a willingness to start writing your story by approaching your life differently.

### 1. Put Yourself in the Story

No one stumbles upon significance. We have to be intentional about making our lives matter. That calls for action—and not excuses. Most people don't know this, but it's easier to go from failure to success than from excuses to success.

In a famous study by Victor and Mildred Goertzel published in a book titled *Cradles of Eminence*, the home backgrounds of three hundred highly successful people were investigated. These three hundred people had made it to the top. They were men and women who would be recognized as brilliant in their fields. The list included Franklin D. Roosevelt, Helen Keller, Winston Churchill, Albert Schweitzer, Clara Barton, Gandhi, Albert Einstein, and Sigmund Freud. The intensive investigation into their early home lives yielded some surprising findings:

- Three-fourths of them as children were troubled by poverty, a broken home, or difficult parents who were rejecting, overpossessive, or domineering.
- Seventy-four of the eighty-five writers of fiction or drama and sixteen of the twenty poets came from homes where, as children, they saw tense psychological drama played out by their parents.
- Over one-fourth of the sample suffered physical handicaps such as blindness, deafness, or crippled limbs.[3]

Adversity tried to knock these people out of their stories, but they didn't allow it to. Why? They were highly intentional. They had a strong *why*—a purpose—which drew them forward even if the road wasn't wide and smooth. (I'll tell you about finding your *why* in chapter four.)

Look at the lives of people who have achieved significance, and you can hear them calling you to put yourself into your story. Perhaps they didn't use those exact words, but if you look at what they've said, you can sense the call to action:

*"To dare is to lose one's footing momentarily. Not to dare is to lose oneself."*

—Søren Kierkegaard

*"If you aren't in over your head, how do you know how tall you are?"*

—T. S. Eliot

*"Be the change you want to see in the world."*

—Mahatma Gandhi

*"Here's to the crazy ones. The misfits. The rebels. The troublemakers. The round pegs in the square holes.*

*The ones who see things differently.... Because the
people who are crazy enough to think they can change
the world are the ones who do."*

—STEVE JOBS

People ask me all the time for advice about how
to write a book. I tell them to start writing. Many
people would love to write a story, a poem, or even
a book, but they never do. Why? They're afraid to
start.

To have a life that matters, you have to start.
Start with yourself. Your *best* story begins when you
put yourself back into it. Be in the picture. Stop
looking—start living! Not only will that change your
life and help others, but it will also give you the credibility and moral authority to inspire and team with
others to make a difference. (I'll talk a lot about this
throughout the book.)

Once, while walking through the Orlando Science
Center, I read these words on a sign: "Experiment—
Experience—Explore. *Do not touch* isn't in our vocab-
ulary." I love that philosophy, not only for a science
center, but also for life. Dive in! You never know how
well you can swim until you are in over your head.

## 2. Put Significance in Your Story

A well-written story is built using elements that people think are important. When we live for significance, we are telling people around us that it is important to us. Almost everyone wants to live a life of meaning and significance, whether or not they express the desire.

To put significance in our stories, we must do things out of our comfort zone. And we must make changes that we may find difficult. We often avoid trying to make those changes. But know this: though not everything that we face can be changed, nothing can be changed until we face it.

To put significance in our stories, we must also take action. Being passive may feel safe. If you do nothing, nothing can go wrong. But while inaction cannot fail, it cannot succeed either. We can wait, and hope, and wish, but if we do, we miss the stories our lives could be.

We cannot allow our fears and questions to keep us from starting. Are you tempted to wait until an ideal time? Do you worry that if you start on this journey without knowing exactly where it will go you might not do well? Are you concerned that you might fail?

Let me help you by telling you something you need to know. You won't do well the first time you do anything. You don't know what you're doing when you start. Nobody is good at the beginning of doing something new. Get over it. Novelist Ernest Hemingway said, "The first draft is always crap." (Only he didn't say *crap*!) And he was awarded the Nobel Prize for Literature. If you want to live a life that matters, don't start when you get good; start now so you become good. I've never known a star athlete who started out good. All start out as beginners, and with practice, some become good. Others become great.

> If you want to live a life that matters, don't start when you get good; start now so you become good.

Everyone starts out bad, regardless of what they're practicing for. We start so we can improve. We start before we're ready because we need and want to get better. The idea is to deliver our best each time we try until one day, we become good. And then one day, we may even have a chance to be great. That's growth. But we can't evolve if we don't start.

Your story won't be perfect. A lot of things will change. But your heart will sing. It will sing the song of significance. It will sing, "I am making a difference!" And that will give you satisfaction down to the soul level.

## 3. Put Your Strengths in Your Story

Recently I had an enlightening lunch with Jim Collins, author of *Good to Great*. We were speaking together at an event in Las Vegas, and after catching up for a few minutes, we began to talk about the meaning and impact of significance.

"Jim," I asked, "what is required to bring about positive life-change to a community?" I knew he had done a lot of research on the subject of transformational movements, and I was very interested to hear his answer.

"There are three questions you need to ask and answer to test your readiness to be a catalyst for significance," Jim replied. "They are:

- Can you be the best in the world at what you do?
- Are you passionate about what you are doing?
- Do you have the resources to change your world?"

Since our conversation that day, I have spent a lot of time thinking about those questions. Here is what I discovered. The first question is about talent. You have skills and abilities that can help others. Can you be the best in the world using them? Maybe, maybe not. Can you be the best *you* in the world using them? Absolutely! No one else has exactly your skills and experiences, opportunities and obstacles, timing and gifts. You are unique, and have a unique chance to make a difference only you can make—if you're willing to get into your story. Your talent will become the leverage in your life for creating the significance story you want to live.

The second question is about heart. Significance begins in the heart when we desire to make a difference. We see a need. We feel a hurt. We want to help. We act on it. Passion is the soul of significance. It's the fuel. It's the core.

The third question is about tools. No doubt you already have many resources at your disposal. My desire is that this book will be another one. It will show you the way so that you can become highly intentional and live a life that matters according to your heart and values.

## 4. Stop Trying and Start Doing

"I'll try my best." This is a statement most of us have made at one time or another. It's a way of saying, "I'll work at having the right attitude and I'll work at the task, but I won't take responsibility for the outcome." But is *trying* to do your best enough for a life of significance? Can we move from where we are to where we want to be just by *trying*?

I don't think so.

*Trying* alone does not communicate true commitment. It's halfhearted. It is not a pledge to do what's necessary to achieve a goal. It's another way of saying, "I'll make an effort." That's not many steps away from, "I'll go through the motions." *Trying* rarely achieves anything significant.

If an attitude of *trying* is not enough, then what is?

An attitude of *doing*!

There is enormous magic in the tiny word *do*. When we tell ourselves, "I'll do it," we unleash tremendous power. That act forges in us a chain of personal responsibility that ups our game: a desire to excel plus a sense of duty plus complete aliveness plus total dedication to getting done what has to be done. That equals commitment.

An attitude of *doing* also helps us to become who we were meant to be. It is this *doing* attitude that often leads to the things we were meant to do. While *trying* is filled with good intentions, *doing* is the result of intentional living.

As you read this, you may be thinking, *I'm not sure if I'm ready to make such a commitment.* Steven Pressfield, author of *The War of Art*, identifies this reluctance. He calls it *resistance*. He writes, "There is a force resisting the beautiful things in the world, and too many of us are giving in." An attitude of *doing* helps us break through that resisting force, and the world needs that. It needs for us to live our stories and contribute to the greater story that's happening around us.

## Discoveries in Your Story of Significance

I hope you will take steps to put yourself fully into your story and begin writing your life of significance—or to increase your significance if you're already doing significant work. From the moment you start, it will have a positive, lasting effect on you. If you're still not sure if you're ready to take that first step, let me help by telling you what it will do for you:

### It Will Change You

What is the number one catalyst for change? It's *action.* Understanding may be able to change minds, but action changes lives. If you take action, it will change your life. And that change will begin changing others.

Entrepreneur and speaker Jim Rohn said, "One of the best places to start to turn your life around is by doing whatever appears on your mental, 'I should' list." What task to help others keeps popping up on your "I should" list? I want to challenge you to develop the discipline of *doing* in that area. Every time we choose action over ease we develop an increasing level of self-worth, self-respect, and self-confidence. In the final analysis, it is often how we feel about ourselves that provides the greatest reward from any activity.

In life, it is not what we *get* that makes us valuable. It is what we *become* in the process that brings value to our lives. Action is what converts human dreams into significance. It brings personal value that we can gain from no other source.

> **Action is what converts human dreams into significance.**

When I was in college, I felt that I should do something positive in the poorest section of the city where I lived. Often I would hear others say that something should be done to help the people who lived there, but I didn't see anyone doing anything about it. So I decided to lead a clean-up effort in that area. For one month, volunteers did work to spruce up the neighborhood. Then we began helping the people who needed medical assistance. Soon people began to take ownership of the neighborhood and things began to change. I vividly remember walking through that area with a great deal of pride of accomplishment. I was full of joy knowing that I had been part of a group of people who had made a difference in that community. As a result, the change inside of me was as great as the change in the neighborhood.

When you take responsibility for your story and intentionally live a life of significance, how will you change?

- *You will reaffirm your values.* Acting on what you value will clarify those values and make them a permanent priority in your life.
- *You will find your voice.* Taking action will give you confidence to speak and live out what you believe in front of others. You will begin to develop a moral authority with people.
- *You will develop your character.* Passive people allow their character to be influenced by others. Active people struggle to form and maintain their character. They grow and develop because of that struggle.
- *You will experience inner fulfillment.* Contentment is found in being where you are supposed to be. It's found when your actions are aligned with who you are.

When we live our lives intentionally for others, we begin to see the world through eyes other than our own, and that inspires us to do more than belong;

we participate. We do more than care; we help. We go beyond being fair; we are kind. We go beyond dreaming; we work. Why? Because we want to make a difference.

If you want a better life, become intentional about your story. The return you get personally will knock your socks off. That doesn't mean it will be smooth sailing. Significance is messy. It's inconvenient. It's overwhelming. At times I've been disappointed in myself. I've also been disappointed by others. All the couldn'ts, didn'ts, and wouldn'ts in my life have shown me my shortcomings. The story I wanted to write and the one being written are different. But that's OK. My strikeouts have developed my character, and my hits have been unforgettable. When your story of significance moves from ideal to real, it will begin to remake you.

## It Will Bring Others into Your Story

What you move toward moves toward you. For years I have taught that when a person moves toward his or her vision, resources begin to move toward that person. Those resources may be materials, money, or people. When a person stops moving, so do the resources. As you step into your story of significance and take action, you will find this to be true.

I have taken this principle one step further. When I move in an area of significance, I also ask people to join me. (I'll explain this in detail in chapter seven.) There's great power in inviting others to join you. You can share significance by inviting others to be part of your story. Don Miller illustrates this in *A Million Miles in a Thousand Years*. He writes,

When we were in Uganda, I went with [my friend] Bob to break ground on a new school he was building. The school board was there, along with the local officials. The principal of the school had bought three trees that Bob, the government official, and the principal would plant to commemorate the breaking of the ground. Bob saw me standing off, taking pictures of the event, and walked over and asked if I would plant his tree for him.

"Are you sure?" I asked.

"Absolutely," he said. "It would be great for me to come back to this place and see the tree you planted, to be reminded of you every time I visit."

I put down my camera and helped dig the hole and set the tree into the ground, covering it to its tiny trunk. And from that moment on, the school was no longer Bob's school; the better story was no longer Bob's story. It was my story, too. I'd entered into the story with Bob. And it's a great story about providing an education to children who would otherwise go without. After that I donated funds to Bob's work in Uganda, and I'm even working to provide a scholarship to a child I met in a prison in Kampala who Bob and his lawyers helped free. I'm telling a better story with Bob.[4]

When you invite others to join you, you both change and have better stories to show for it. As poet Edwin Markham wrote,

*There is a destiny that makes us brothers*
*None goes his way alone.*
*All that we send into the lives of others*
*Comes back into our own.*

My greatest memories have come from the times others were in my story of significance with me. There is no joy that can equal that of people working together for common good. Today, my best friends are those who are taking the significance journey with me. Those friendships are heightened by meaningful experiences. Yours will be, too.

## It Will Increase Your Appetite for More Significance

In 2013 at a speaking engagement I had in Bahrain, I sat across the table from Jaap Vaandrager at lunch. He is a highly successful businessman from the Netherlands who lives and works in Bahrain. During our conversation he asked me what I was writing. I briefly shared that I was writing this book about making a difference. He responded, "My daughter Celine is making a difference in the lives of people, and she is only a teenager." He started to tell me her story, and I was blown away by it.

Growing up in the Netherlands, Celine knew how privileged she was. This became clear to her in India. Her father and grandfather had done many charity projects there, and she had gone there herself and witnessed the conditions. "I have seen how many people live in extreme poverty," said Celine. "The children in the slums and other less fortunate areas lack basic education, and the only language they learn is the local language, which limits their opportunities later in life. Their greatest wish is to break out of the slums and start a life in the city with a stable job, a stable income, and a loving family."

The key, she realized, was education. "I believe that it is one of the most important things in life and it enables people to do whatever they desire with their life," said Celine. She thought that if children could be taught English, they would have a chance at a better life as they grew up.

Celine had a plan. She would provide underprivileged children at a school with an English teacher. That would help them later in life and provide greater opportunities for them. After doing a lot of research and with the help of her friends in India, she found a school. It needed an English teacher, but didn't have enough money to pay for one. At this school and others like it, students received only the most basic supplies and a lunch, which for many is the only hot meal they get all day.

The school she found was called Mahadji Shinde Primary School. The children who attended, forty-four to a class, were some of the least fortunate children in all of India: 10 percent were orphans, 60 percent had only one parent, and 80 percent lived in sheds in the slums.

Finding an English teacher for the school was not easy, but Celine did it in a month. The teacher was a young single woman whose entire family depended on her salary, including her father, who had cancer. She had been unemployed and was grateful for the job. Now all Celine had to do was figure out how to pay her.

She began raising money by holding bake sales at her school. She also sponsored swims. But the amount of money was nowhere near enough to fulfill her aims.

As Celine's sixteenth birthday approached, she knew what she wanted to do. "For my sixteenth birthday I stepped it up a notch, inviting all my friends, family's friends, and classmates to come to a birthday fundraiser I was having and I told them to bring a plus one."

Instead of asking for gifts, she asked for donations for a charity she was creating called No Nation Without Education.

"Within hours the whole donation box was filled and I already knew I had achieved my target," said Celine. "When I counted up the money I couldn't believe my eyes. We had gone over more than double the money required. Success!"

She used the money to pay the teacher's salary for a year. That meant the children would get English lessons, and the teacher would have a stable job for a year and her father's cancer would be treated. With the extra money, Celine bought dozens of basic English books for the children and stuffed animals for the primary school. When Celine went there to deliver the books and toys, the children were overjoyed and welcomed her enthusiastically. On the same trip, she helped with other projects her grandfather had sponsored.

"I had such a fantastic time in India," said Celine. "I couldn't thank everyone enough for helping me. It was a life-changing experience and one I will never forget."

But Celine's story doesn't end there. She says, "My new mission? To build a school in Mumbai, India, for my eighteenth birthday."

Celine's story shows that when you make significance a part of your story, it only increases your appetite to do more things that matter. I know that once I started adding value to others, it became an obsession in the best sense of the word. The more I did it, the more I became intentional in finding other opportunities. A butterfly cannot go back to being a caterpillar. When you start living the significance story, you get a taste for making a difference and you won't go back.

> A butterfly cannot go back to being a caterpillar. When you start living the significance story, you get a taste for making a difference and you won't go back.

I wish I had read a story like Celine's when I was a teenager. Even with all of the advantages I had, no one ever pointed out that there were people doing significant things at that age. And it never occurred to me that I could make such a difference as a kid. Knowing this possibility then would have had a huge impact on me.

## It Will Outlive You

In my book *The Leadership Handbook*, there is a chapter on legacy titled "People Will Summarize Your Life in One Sentence—Pick It Now." By getting into your story and becoming intentional about making a difference, you can choose your legacy. What an opportunity! Today you and I can decide to live a life that matters, and that will impact how we will be remembered after we're gone.

My wife, Margaret, was deeply moved by a book called *Forget-Me-Not: Timeless Sentiments for Lifelong Friends*, by Janda Sims Kelley. It is a collection of prose and poetry written in the 1800s. One of the entries particularly impacted her. It said,

*To Viola,*
*Dare to do right, dare to be true,*
*You have a work that*
*no other can do.*
*Do it so kindly,*
*so bravely, so well,*
*That angels will hasten*
*the story to tell.*
*Your friend, Annie*
*Haskinville, New York, February 08, 1890*

Isn't that what all of us should strive to do? As Viktor Frankl said, "Everyone has his own specific vocation or mission in life. Everyone must carry out a concrete assignment that demands fulfillment. Therein he cannot be replaced, nor can his life be repeated. Thus everyone's task is as unique as his specific opportunity to implement it."

## This Is Personal

At this point, I should pause so that I can tell you something. If you've read any of my previous books, you're going to find this one different in both tone and approach. I will show you the way to intentional living and help you to create your own life that matters, but I'm also going to tell you a lot of my personal story—from growing up and going to school in small-town Ohio during the fifties and sixties; to becoming the pastor of a tiny church in rural Indiana; to leading ever-growing churches through the seventies, eighties, and nineties; to crossing over as a speaker to teach businesspeople and leaders; to starting several businesses and a nonprofit organization; to eventually training millions of leaders around the world.

I won't be telling you all this to toot my own horn. My life is flawed, yet I believe I need to share it with you in a way I never have before because I don't know of any better way to teach you how to embark upon intentional living. I believe that if you know my story and how it unfolded, it will help you to write your own story of significance. It will empower you to lead yourself to a life that matters.

Let me also tell you something else. I talk pretty openly about my faith in this book. I do that because it has been an important part of my personal journey. It may also be a part of yours. But I also know that it may not be. Rest assured, I will not try to force my faith on you. If you're indifferent to faith, or even if you have a negative disposition toward faith or God, I sincerely believe you'll benefit from hearing my story. Having said that, I want you to know that I'll let you know when I'm going to talk about my faith, and you can skip that section if you want to. I won't be offended.

Since it's confession time, I'll also let you in on a little secret. I struggled with writing this book— more than with any book I've ever written. Why? The message of intentional living and the resulting significance is so meaningful, so powerful, and so very personal that I felt I had to get it right. I believe what I have to say on this subject has the potential to change your life, as it has mine.

And to help you start taking your first steps into significance right away, I've created something called the seven-day experiment. It will show you how to take your first small steps in your journey of intentional living and significance. Go to 7DayExperiment.com and try it out. It's free.

As I have looked back at my story and explored my journey of intentional living and significance, I have come to realize that it followed a pattern, a pattern I will use to show you the way. Here it is:

*I Want to Make a Difference*
*Doing Something That Makes a Difference,*
*With People Who Make a Difference,*
*At a Time That Makes a Difference.*

The rest of the book is organized in alignment with the pattern of those four thoughts (after I explain some things about intentional living in the next chapter). My desire is that as you read and hear about me, you will make discoveries about yourself, your calling to make a difference, and about your ability to live a life of significance, which you can start doing now.

Even though I will be telling you much of my story, and revealing more about my background than I ever have, I want you to understand that my story isn't more important than anyone else's—including yours. I believe that every person has great value. Every person matters. I believe in you. I believe in your potential for personal transformation. And I believe you have the ability to make an impact on the world.

Your story, like mine, won't be perfect. Everyone's story includes wins and losses, good days and bad, highs and lows, surprises and uncertainties. That's life. This book is not about creating a *perfect* life for you. It's about wanting a *better* life for you.

I've been an observer of people all my life, and I've noticed that most people are pretty passive about their lives. An indication of this is that when asked to describe significant regrets in their lives, eight out of ten people focus on actions they did *not* take rather than actions they *did*. In other words, they focus on things they failed *to* do rather than things they failed *at* doing. A better story will emerge for you when you are highly intentional with your life. I know because I have experienced it.

## Your Best Story

One of my favorite movies is *Amistad,* directed by Steven Spielberg. It's about a mutiny on a slave ship and the trial that occurred to determine the status of the rebellious slaves after the vessel miraculously made it to the United States. Representing the slaves was African American abolitionist lawyer Theodore Joadson, played by Morgan Freeman. His advisor was former US president John Quincy Adams, played by Anthony Hopkins.

In the movie, Adams asks Joadson to summarize his case. Joadson's summary is brilliant, accurate, and devoid of emotion. Old Adams then counsels Joadson: "Early in my career in the law, I learned that *whoever tells the best story wins.*"

I want you to win by telling the best story you can with your life.

As you think about your life story and how you want it ultimately to read, I want to leave you with a final thought. I often teach that we have two great tasks in life: to find ourselves and to lose ourselves. Ultimately, I believe we find ourselves by discovering our *why*. We lose ourselves while traveling the path of significance by putting others first. The result? The people we help also find themselves, and the legacy cycle can begin again. That cycle has the power to live on after us. When I die, I cannot take with me what I have, but I can live in others by what I gave. This is what I hope for you as you read this book.

> When I die, I cannot take with me what I have, but I can live in others by what I gave.

If you're ready to learn how living with intentionality will change your life, then turn the page and let's look at why having good intentions alone is never enough for living a life of significance.

## Intentional Application:
## Your Life Can Be a Great Story

### Your Story So Far

How would you characterize your life story so far? Is it already a great one? Is it good, but not spectacular? Is it falling short of what you want it to be? Take some time to think about it by writing about it. You can do that any number of ways. You can create a list of every memorable moment—both positive and negative. You can write it out as a story. You can jot down ideas or create a summary paragraph. The how isn't that important. What matters is that you take the time to do it, and be sure to think about whether your story is headed in the direction you want it to go by the time you're done living.

### Start Outlining a New Chapter

If the direction of your life isn't all that you want it to be, then take some time to write out what you want to accomplish to make the world a better place. It doesn't need to be lofty. It doesn't have to be earth-shattering. It just needs to make a difference in some way that's important to you. What would you like people to say at your funeral? Write it now.

## Step into Your Story

Now try to discern what it would mean for you to become more proactive in making your life matter and stepping into your own story. Identify what single action you could take today and every day for the next week or month to start rewriting your own story. As Doug Horton says, "Be your own hero. It's cheaper than a movie ticket."

# 2

## Why Good Intentions Aren't Enough

Poet Samuel Johnson is credited with saying, "Hell is paved with good intentions." Why would he say such a thing? Isn't it a positive thing to want to do good, to possess a desire to help others? My answer is yes. Having a heart to help people and add value to them makes you a better person. But if you don't act on it in an intentional way, it won't make a difference.

### Crossing the Significance Gap

In the movie *Pay It Forward*, teacher Eugene Simonet challenges his class to go out and make a difference in the lives of others. "Think of an idea to change our world, then put it into action," he tells his students. Why? Because he knows that most people, even though they desire to do something that matters, don't start intentionally building the bridge between knowing and doing. They wait. As a result, they never span the gap. And as a result, they never experience significance.

When I look back at my own journey of significance, I recognize that it began with good intentions more than intentional living. My good intentions expressed my heart and desire to help others but fell far short of the significance I genuinely craved. A great example of this occurred when I was in high school. I loved basketball growing up. From junior high school on, I played on the basketball team, and I was pretty good. But I always wanted to play football, too. However, I knew my parents didn't want me to play two sports. They worried I wouldn't be able to keep up with my studies. So I had a dilemma. Every summer, I told my buddies I would be at football tryouts that fall. It was my *intention* to show up. However, I knew I'd disappoint my parents if I did. So inevitably, I disappointed myself and my friends by not going. The result was that my intentions were inconsistent with my behavior.

Early in my life, too many times my intentions were just thoughts—great ideas but not backed with actions. If I had just been *intentional* and told my parents I wanted to play football, I think they would have let me.

The sad part is that I never got to play football because I never told them how I felt. Every fall, I sat in the stands watching the game because that's as far as my good intentions took me. Over time I found a way to get out of the stands and onto the field more often in life. It came as I began to see the difference between *good intentions* and *intentional living*. Significance only started to become mine when I became consciously aware of the need to take action and follow through every single day.

What game are you watching that you'd rather be playing? Are you sitting in the stands in areas of your life where you could be making a difference?

> **What game are you watching that you'd rather be playing?**

There are many ways to be significant—as many as there are people on earth. Each of us has unique skills, talents, opportunities, causes, and callings. I'll help you start to figure out what some of those things are for you in subsequent chapters. But there is only one certain pathway for you to achieve that significance, and that's through intentional living. Since you're still reading this book, I believe you have made the decision to get into your story as I suggested in chapter one. You want to live a life that matters. You desire significance. That's good. But the next question is how.

First, let me clarify what I mean when I talk about *intentional living*. I'm describing a life that brings you *daily satisfaction* and *continual rewards* for merely working to make a difference—small or large—in the lives of others. Intentional living is the bridge that will lead you to a life that matters. Good intentions won't get you there.

What's the big difference between good intentions and intentional living? I can show you using just a few words. Take a look at the three columns of words below, and as you do, ask yourself, "Do I live in the land of good intentions, or in the land of intentional living?"

| WORDS OF GOOD INTENTION | WORDS OF INTENTIONAL LIVING | A LIFE THAT MATTERS |
|---|---|---|
| Desire | Action | Results |
| Wish | Purpose | Fulfillment |
| Someday | Today | Every Day |
| Fantasy | Strategy | Follow-Through |
| Hopefully | Definitely | Continually |
| Passive | Active | Proactive |
| Occasional | Continual | Habitual |
| Emotion | Discipline | Lifestyle |
| Somebody Should | I Will | I Do |
| Survival | Success | Significance |

As you look at these lists, can you see why good intentions alone will never get you to significance? In fact, if all you ever do is cultivate good intentions, but you never act with intentionality, you're actually likely to become more frustrated and less fulfilled, because your desire for positive change may increase, but the lack of results will leave you frustrated.

Whether we realize it or not, people live in one land or the other. Whether by design or default, if we have a desire to make the world a better place, we either settle for good intentions or embrace intentional living. Which will you do?

## Learning to Be Intentional

Even someone like me, who grew up in a home where intentionality was highly valued, doesn't always understand how to be intentional right off the bat.

My father is the most intentional person I've ever met. He knows what he believes, he identifies what he wants, he thinks about what he needs to do to bring about the results he wants, and he consistently takes action to see it through. He's in his nineties, and he's still living intentionally.

As a young man, Dad studied successful people

and found they all had one thing in common: a positive attitude. He was not a naturally positive person, so he began reading books and listening to speakers who taught him how to become more positive. And he practiced positive thinking every day. He still does.

Here's another example of his intentionality. During the Depression, when many people were out of work, he would go to a business where he hoped to get a job, and he would work a day for free. He figured that his work would be so good that the business owner would simply hire him on the spot. If that didn't happen, he would move on and do the same thing for another business. He was never out of work.

My parents were highly intentional with my older brother Larry, my younger sister Trish, and me. Because they wanted to meet our friends and supervise us as we built relationships, they made sure we had everything kids could ever want at our house: toys, a Ping-Pong table, a chemistry set, and a pool table. As a result, all the neighborhood kids gathered there, and my mother would gently guide us about which relationships were positive and which were negative.

At the dinner table, my mom and dad would ask questions every night. "What did you read today? What did you try and fail at?" My parents were trying to plant seeds of intentionality in us at every meal.

Dad was intentional about our growth and development, too. He paid us for reading books he knew would improve us, instead of paying us to put out the garbage. (I still put out the garbage. I just didn't get paid for it!) And the day I got my driver's license, before we got in the car to go home, he said, "I'm going to teach you the most important lesson you'll ever learn about driving." He pulled a book from his jacket pocket, and put it in the glove box. "There will be times when you're stopped in traffic, stuck at a train track, or waiting for someone," he said. "The best way to use that time and make it count is to read." My love of reading was intentionally instilled in me by my dad.

Despite my parents' high degree of intentionality, I didn't really get it as a kid. I didn't embrace intentional living. Maybe there was too much play in me. Mostly, I wanted to have fun. Then when I became an adult, I thought hard work was the key to success. I believed that the harder you worked, the more successful you would be.

What changed me? How did I finally recognize that intentional living was the key to a life that matters, that it was the bridge between success and significance? When I was in my midtwenties, I met a man named Curt Kampmeier.

Curt was associated with the Success Motivation

Institute out of Waco, Texas. Because I had heard him talk about the principles of success and I really liked what he had to say, I had written him a note asking to meet with him the next time he came through my town. Much to my surprise, he said yes. So we met for breakfast.

While I was eating my eggs, Curt asked me if I had a personal plan for growth for my life. It was a question nobody had ever asked me. Not only didn't I have one, I didn't even know I was supposed to have one. I was so embarrassed by the question that I tried to fake my response. I started to tell him about all the things I was doing in my work and how many hours I put in. He saw right through it.

"If you're going to grow," he said, "you have to be intentional."

> **"If you're going to grow, you have to be intentional."**
>
> —*Curt Kampmeier*

That statement hit me like a punch in the face.

Curt told me he had a detailed plan for growth—a kit with material on goals and attitude and initiative and responsibility. I knew instinctively that these things could help me. When I asked him how I could get it, he told me I could purchase it for $695.

That was the equivalent of one month's salary for me!

I went home from breakfast looking for alternatives. I started asking friends and colleagues if they had a plan for growth. Nope. None of my friends was intentional about becoming better at what he did. They just expected it to happen on its own, like I had. That sounds kind of like good intentions, doesn't it?

Finally, my wife, Margaret, and I sat down, put pencil to paper, and figured out how to sacrifice and pinch our pennies to save the money to buy the kit. We were newly married then, barely scraping by on the money we were making. Yet at the end of six months, we'd saved what we needed. (Realize that this was in the days before credit cards were available to everyone.)

I'll never forget the day I received the kit. I had seen it before when I met with Curt, but when I opened it and started to dig into it, I was struck by the simplicity of it. At first I thought, *I paid almost $700 for this?* I had been hoping for a silver bullet. Instead, this was going to require a lot of work.

What else could I do? I dove in. After all, we'd spent a small fortune for the kit. But it wasn't long before I realized it was worth every penny. Yes, it encouraged me to dream, but it also taught me to put details to my dreams and attach deadlines to them. It prompted me to examine myself and where I was. It called me to look at my strengths and weaknesses. It made me identify my goals every week. And it engaged me in a process of growth every day.

I had hoped for a solution. Instead, it gave me direction.

It was a course in intentional living. Even buying the kit had forced me to be intentional, because we had made sacrifices every day for six months to save the money.

That kit opened my eyes to intentional living. It helped me begin creating my first life plan. I cannot put a price on how valuable it was. Why? Because it led to a major epiphany:

If I wanted to make a difference...

> *Wishing for things to change wouldn't make them change.*
> *Hoping for improvements wouldn't bring them.*
> *Dreaming wouldn't provide all the answers I needed.*
> *Vision wouldn't be enough to bring transformation to me or others.*
> *Only by managing my thinking and shifting my thoughts from desire to deeds would I be able to bring about positive change. I needed to go from wanting to doing.*

Maybe you've already had this epiphany yourself. Maybe you've already begun to make this shift. Maybe you figured it out earlier than I did. But if you didn't, guess what? You can make the change from good intentions to intentional living right now. In fact, you can become so intentional in the way you live that your friends and loved ones, your colleagues and bosses, your neighbors and naysayers will say, "What in the world happened?" Your transformation will blow their minds. And it will inspire others to embrace intentional living, too.

## The Seven Benefits of Intentional Living

Intuitively, you might sense that intentional living would benefit you, but I'm guessing you'd also like to know specifically what it does for us. My experience has shown me that it does many things for us. Here are seven of its benefits:

### 1. Intentional Living Prompts Us to Ask, "What Is Significant in My Life?"

I was twenty-five years old when I met Curt Kampmeier, and I desperately wanted to be successful. Working through his kit and becoming intentional prompted me to begin asking, "What are the keys to success?" For the next eighteen months, I studied successful people and started forming ideas based on the information I was gathering.

After observing dozens of successful people and reading many books, I came to a conclusion: *Successful people are good in four areas: relationships, equipping, attitude, and leadership.* Those were the areas I would need to cultivate if I wanted to become successful. With a growth plan formulated, I began developing myself in those four areas.

Living intentionally will motivate you to start asking questions and begin prioritizing whatever is important to you. That's what it did for me. I began by asking how I could be successful. When I had begun to achieve some success, I realized that I needed to be asking questions about significance. *Can I make a difference? Whom should I help? How can I help them? How can I add value to them?* These questions began to help me become intentional in the area of significance.

Once I asked myself, "What is significant in my life?" and realized the answer was adding value to people, I began to focus on that thought. That's the essence of intentionality. An unintentional life accepts everything and does nothing. An intentional life embraces only the things that will add to the mission of significance.

> An unintentional life accepts everything and does nothing. An intentional life embraces only the things that will add to the mission of significance.

## 2. Intentional Living Motivates Us to Take Immediate Action in Areas of Significance

When you have shifted from good intentions to intentional living, whenever you detect a need that matters to you, you no longer think, *Something must be done about that.* Instead, you think, *I must do something about that.* You take ownership. Napoleon Hill said it best when he observed, "You must get involved to have an impact. No one is impressed with the won-lost record of a referee."

My shift toward intentional living was amplified in my midtwenties when I heard W. Clement Stone speak at a positive-motivational-attitude rally in Dayton, Ohio. He was a student of Napoleon Hill, whose books I had read, so I was very eager to hear what Stone had to say.

One of the lessons he taught that day was about the need to create urgency to get things done. He challenged us to say aloud to ourselves fifty times every morning before we got out of bed, "Do it now. Do it now. Do it now." Every evening before we went to sleep, he challenged us to once again to say the phrase, "Do it now," fifty times.

He told us to do this exercise every day for one month until it became a discipline.

I left that conference and heeded his advice. I actually

did it. Every day. Fifty times in the morning and fifty in the evening. At the end of that month I had within me such a sense of urgency to act that I found myself ready to seize the moment at any time. This new, "do it now" mentality caused me to live with such immense anticipation that I began to take action on all of the things I had been delaying. It took me to a whole new level.

We all have a tendency to put off things. I needed the "do it now" exercise to get me motivated to do acts of significance. It began as a discipline, but it turned into a daily delight. It quickly transcended from "I have to" to "I want to" to "I can't wait to." (I'll talk about this in greater detail in chapter nine.) No people have ever thought themselves into significance. They acted themselves into it. You can't sit in the bleachers as I did in high school—you've got to get in the game.

Allow the desire to act that you feel when you become intentional to propel you into acts of significance. The most important thing you can do is to get started because it will increase your appetite for more significance.

### 3. Intentional Living Challenges Us to Find Creative Ways to Achieve Significance

When I was in college, I scored below average in a creativity test given to me and my classmates. Yet, I have been able to deliver thousands of messages and write dozens of books that have been well received by people. How was I able to change? When I became intentional in what I wanted to do, I became creative in finding ways to obtain my desires. A clear picture of what I wanted to accomplish gave me the will to persist and the creative spirit to overcome barriers and make up for deficiencies.

When you live an intentional lifestyle, you see many possibilities. When you are unintentional, you see few:

Intentional living always has an idea.
Unintentional living always has an excuse.

Intentional living fixes the situation.
Unintentional living fixes the blame.

Intentional living makes it happen.
Unintentional living wonders what happened.

Intentional living says, "Here's something I can do."
Unintentional living says, "Why doesn't someone else do something?"

Intentional and unintentional living are worlds apart in every aspect of life, including creativity.

Intentional living is all about knowing what you

want. Often that desire will be elusive or even seemingly impossible to achieve. However, when we feel that way, necessity disguised as creativity can kick in. When it does, intentional living turns the doubt-filled question "Can I?" into the invigorating, possibility-inducing *"How* can I?" When you know what you want and can't find what you need, you must create what you need, so you can get what you want!

> When you know what you want and can't find what you need, you must create what you need, so you can get what you want!

## 4. Intentional Living Energizes Us to Give Our Best Effort to Do Significant Acts

Best-selling author Bob Moawad said, "Most people don't aim too high and miss. They aim too low and hit." What's even worse than that? Not aiming at all!

> "Most people don't aim too high and miss. They aim too low and hit."
> —Bob Moawad

Being unintentional is failing to take aim in life. Unintentional people wander through life without focus. They are like Brother Juniper in the comic strip by Father Justin "Fred" McCarthy, who shoots arrows at a wooden fence in the backyard. He pulls back the bowstring and lets the arrow fly. Wherever it sticks into the fence, he takes a marker and draws a target around it. This way, he figures he is sure never to miss a bull's-eye.

Sadly, many people live their lives similarly, landing somewhere random and calling it a bull's-eye. That describes life without purpose or energy. Living that way would be like golfing without the hole, playing football without the goal line, playing baseball without home plate, or bowling without the pins.

I became aware of the necessity of goals at ten years old, though I didn't recognize the significance at the time. I fell in love with basketball at that age. My father wanted to provide me with a place to play at home, so he poured a concrete drive and put a backboard on the garage. He and I then went to town and bought a basketball and a rim. I was so excited, because I was about to have my very own place where I could practice basketball every day.

Dad was about to put up the rim on the backboard when he received an emergency call and had to leave on a trip. At that time Dad was a superintendent who was responsible for leading many pastors. Sometimes a crisis situation needing his immediate attention would occur, so I understood well when he had one of these sudden departures.

"John," he said, "when I get back home tomorrow, I will put up your rim."

"No problem," I replied. "I'll practice until you get back."

As he backed the car out of the driveway, I waved goodbye and then started dribbling my new ball on the fresh concrete drive. After about fifteen minutes of dribbling I got bored. So I decided to throw the ball against the backboard. I thought it would satisfy me. But it didn't. As the ball bounced off the backboard and rolled to the side of the driveway, I lost all interest in playing. What was basketball without the basket? Just dribbling. And dribbling the ball wasn't what the game was all about. Scoring is the ultimate purpose of the game, and there's no scoring without the hoop.

This is symbolic of many things in life. For anything to have great meaning, it needs to be driven by a specific objective and followed through with action. We know this when we're trying to win the one we love before we get married. When we're dating, the pursuit of the other person is usually highly intentional. We try to maximize every experience with the person. We do extra things and go out of our way to please him or her. We look our best. We're on our best behavior. We try to make our loved one's day. Sadly, after the marriage, many people lose that intentionality and focus on the other person, and they spend their time waiting for the other person to make their day. That's when the relationship begins to slide.

Of course, intentionality can take us in the wrong direction when our focus is off. I learned that on my wedding day. After the ceremony, Margaret and I were packing the car to leave for our honeymoon. We planned to drive to Florida to stay at her grandparents' house for a week. As I was loading our luggage, Margaret saw me placing not one but *two* briefcases in the trunk.

"What are those, John?" she asked.

"I thought I'd bring along some work to do in my spare time," I said, pleased with myself for being so strategic.

"Honey, there'll be no spare time!" she said with a curious combination of irritation and flirtation. I'd tell you she was right, but that's none of your business! Let's just say that as we packed the car, she was already trying to teach me an important lesson in intentional living.

## 5. Intentional Living Unleashes the Power of Significance within Us

I was around twenty-six years old when I first saw Zig Ziglar speak. I was sitting in the middle seat of the front row of an auditorium, doing my best to glean everything I could from this master of motivation. I was deeply drawn to his upbeat attitude, his easygoing, conversational style, and his friendly and approachable southern drawl. As he spoke and moved across the stage, I felt as if he were talking to just me, even though I was part of an audience of ten thousand people.

It was during this speech that I heard Zig say, "If you will first help others get what they want, they will help you get what you want." And I experienced another major significance epiphany. I realized that up until then, I had been putting myself and my needs ahead of others. I was always focused on my agenda and what I wanted to accomplish, not on others and what was important to them. I cared about people, but it had never occurred to me that focusing on others and helping them would actually help *me*.

> "If you will first help others get what they want, they will help you get what you want."
>
> —Zig Ziglar

Not only did what Zig said make perfect sense to me, but I knew I could do it. It would be an easy fix. I already liked people. I simply hadn't been aware of my naïve mistake in leadership.

I immediately changed my leadership approach with others, and the response was dramatic. As soon as I expressed genuine interest in people, they reciprocated and showed more interest in me. By putting others first, I was letting them know I believed that their lives mattered. Instead of only selling my vision and motivating people to join my team, I began to first ask about their dreams and how I could help them achieve what they so deeply desired.

As I made this change in my leadership, I was consciously aware I was doing the right thing by putting those I led ahead of myself, and in time I experienced the joy of seeing this truth work in the lives of others. As they received the attention and care they needed, they were not just ready, but also willing and able, to help me fulfill my vision.

It is a law of nature that you cannot reap without sowing. That's why it's so important to give first, before you expect to receive. The compounding, positive result of practicing this principle for many years has now given me an immeasurable return on my investment into people's lives. People are not only making a difference, but they are also investing in others who are making a difference. I'm seeing season after season of harvest in the lives of others.

This give-and-take is natural, like breathing. You take in air; you blow it out. You can never just breathe in. Nor can you just breathe out. Both are continually essential. Likewise, we give to others and receive from them. Our lives are to be like a river, not a reservoir. What we have should flow through us to others. The moment the good things we have to offer begin flowing from ourselves to others, the miracle of intentional significance begins to happen. The more we share, the more we have. The more we have, the more we can give. We don't hand out significance in little doses over time. We unleash it. That's how we build a life that matters.

### 6. Intentional Living Inspires Us to Make Every Day Count

John Wooden, who mentored me for several years, admonished everyone to make every day their masterpiece. This legendary coach of the UCLA Bruins basketball team once explained, "As a leader of my team, it was my responsibility to get the most out of my players. As a coach, I would ask myself every day, 'How can I make my team better?' I concluded that my team would improve when each player improved, and that only would happen when each player each day intentionally made that day his masterpiece."

How did Coach do that? Every day during practice he would watch the energy, focus, and overall behavior of each player. If a player was not giving his best, he would walk over to him and say, "I can tell you are not giving 100 percent of yourself to practice today. I know you are tired, perhaps you stayed up late studying, or maybe this day has been a difficult one. I also know you are thinking, *I'm only giving 60 percent today, but tomorrow I will give 140 percent and make up for today.* I want you to know that thinking will not make you a better player. You cannot give 140 percent tomorrow. The best any of us can give on any day is 100 percent. Therefore, if you give only 60 percent today you will lose 40 percent and never recover it. A few days of less than 100 percent and you will be just an average player."

John Wooden was a master of intentionality when he coached. He planned every practice for his players down to the minute, and wrote that plan out on index cards before the players came together. He once said that if you asked him what his team had done in practice on any given day during his long career, he could retrieve the index card for that day from his files and tell you what all his players were doing. His philosophy was "many hours of planning for a couple hours of practicing." And it worked. His record of ten national titles speaks for itself. No wonder he was named Coach of the Century by *Sports Illustrated*.

Coach's teaching motivated me to write the book *Today Matters*. The thesis of that book states, "The secret of your success is determined by your daily agenda." The key is to make good decisions based on your principles and values, and then to manage those decisions every day. When I wrote that book, I considered the lessons to be simple and basic. But the teachings of John Wooden were simple, too. He focused on fundamentals, yet he was immensely successful. The key is in the consistent follow-through.

A couple of years ago I was speaking in Singapore. While signing books for the group, a young lady handed me *Today Matters* and asked me to sign the back of the book.

"Why the back?" I asked

"Last year I bought this book, and you signed the front," she replied. "I've now read it and mastered the daily dozen you write about. Now I'd like you to sign the back of the book."

As I did, she continued, "You taught me to focus on today, and I've done that. What's the next book that I should read?"

I wish I could have handed her this book, because it would have given her the next step in achieving a life of significance. I have no doubt she would have put the ideas into practice that very day. I could see that she wasn't a person of good intentions. She was already practicing intentional living.

## 7. Intentional Living Encourages Us to Finish Well

On February 20, 2012, I turned sixty-five. As many other people do, I saw this as a significant birthday, and that made me reflective. One of the thoughts that kept recurring in my mind was that I wanted to finish well. For the next six months, I asked myself every day, "How can I finish well?"

What did I mean by that?

I did not want to get to the end of my life and discover I had lived the length of it but without any depth. After much thought, on August 13, 2012, I wrote this:

I Want to Finish Well
Therefore I Will...
Be Bigger on the Inside than the Outside— Character Matters
Follow the Golden Rule—People Matter
Value Humility above All Virtues—Perspective Matters
Travel the High Road of Life—Attitude Matters
Teach Only What I Believe—Passion Matters
Make Every Day My Masterpiece—Today Matters
Love God with All My Being—God Matters
Finish Well—Faithfulness Matters

Nobody finishes well by accident.

Nobody finishes well by accident.

My father is now ninety-three. He is finishing well. Every day he adds value to people. He loves them and serves them. Not long ago I asked, "Dad, what keeps you going?"

His reply: "Every day I try to make a difference for others. That gives me the energy I need to keep going."

Every Sunday Dad leads church services in the assisted-care village where he lives. When he arrived there, he started with just one service. When he filled that one up, he started a second. He filled it up, and now has three full services every Sunday.

Recently he said to me, "John, we keep growing and have run out of room. I'm looking into doing services at satellite locations."

He's ninety-three and thinking about satellite services! Most people his age are thinking about sleep. Where does he get his energy?

Intentional living. Are you getting the picture?

If I'm anything like him—and I hope I am—I still have plenty of time to make a difference. Whenever I ask my dad about his day, he usually talks about someone he has recently helped, encouraged, or inspired. He's going to fully live until he dies, and never get the two confused. I want to be more like him.

Someday I'm going to die. You are, too. What do you want people to say about you at your funeral? I hope people tell funny stories about me. But I also hope they tell a story of significance. I don't want my family and friends to have to guess about my legacy. I want them to tell about how I added value to leaders who multiply value to others. That's the legacy I'm living to create. I believe that's the best contribution I can make while I'm here.

We've all heard the saying, "All's well that ends well," but I believe nothing can end well unless it *starts* well. If you want a life that matters, you don't need to change everything in your life. The shift I am inviting you to make is not huge—but to live a life that matters, it is essential. It is the shift from good intentions to intentional living. That small tweak in your mindset will bring massive significant dividends.

Are you ready to take that step? It's simpler than you might imagine. You just need to align your thinking and your actions. That's what I did. When I recognized I had a choice to be intentional, good intentions no longer ruled my life. You have the power to choose which category to live in, and I want to show you how to get there, how to be intentional and achieve significance.

What will this look like for you? Your journey will probably be similar to mine in some ways. It will be filled with wonderful surprises, great excitement, big changes, unanticipated growth, fond memories, and, hopefully, a tremendous level of inner fulfillment. However, it will also be vastly different from mine. It will be as unique as you are. Significance will be deeply personal and special. I believe becoming highly intentional will be the beginning of a whole new world of opportunity for you.

Most people fear that significance is out of their reach. It's not. Anyone can be significant. You can be significant—but *only* if you begin living intentionally by...

**Wanting to make a difference.** Significance begins with *wanting* to make a difference. If you don't have the desire, you can't be significant.

**Doing something that makes a difference.** When you find your sweet spot—your unique strength that makes a difference—you are able to increase your significance impact.

**Doing something with people who want to make a difference.** Significance compounds when you partner with others. The Law of Significance from *The 17 Indisputable Laws of Teamwork* is true: one is too small a number to achieve greatness.

**Doing something at a time when it makes a difference.** You have to act with a sense of urgency and anticipation if you want to be significant.

When you embrace each of these four elements, you increase your odds and opportunities for significance. If you live out all four of them in your significance journey, you can be assured that you will truly live a life that matters.

The remainder of this book is organized into these four essential elements required to achieve significance through intentional living. They will help you leave mere good intentions behind and shift into a new gear. But before you start reading about them and learn the details of how to take your own significance journey, you have a decision to make.

Are you willing to make the shift from good intentions to intentional living?

If you're not, you might as well stop reading now, because a life of significance won't be possible for you. *Intentional living is the only pathway to significant living.* It is the first step.

If you are willing to make this shift, then let the following pages be your guide to the life you've always wanted but never thought was possible. Once you enter that pathway, your life will really begin to matter to you and to others. Please hear me: Significance is within your grasp. All you need to do is be willing to take the steps.

## Intentional Application:
## Why Good Intentions Aren't Enough

When we make a judgment call about ourselves, we tend to give ourselves the benefit of the doubt. We know what our *intentions* were, so even if we fall short in our execution, we cut ourselves some slack. That's both good and bad. The good is that it allows us to remain positive and bounce back from failure. The bad is that we aren't holding ourselves accountable for following through, and a life of significance is impossible for anyone who doesn't live intentionally day after day.

### Where Do You Fit on the List?

Earlier in this chapter, I introduced you to lists of words that illustrated the differences between good intentions and intentional living. Take another look at them. Put a check next to the word in the left or middle column on each line that better describes your attitude and actions.

| WORDS OF GOOD INTENTION | WORDS OF INTENTIONAL LIVING | A LIFE THAT MATTERS |
|---|---|---|
| Desire | Action | Results |
| Wish | Purpose | Fulfillment |
| Someday | Today | Every Day |
| Fantasy | Strategy | Follow-Through |
| Hopefully | Definitely | Continually |
| Passive | Active | Proactive |
| Occasional | Continual | Habitual |
| Emotion | Discipline | Lifestyle |
| Somebody Should | I Will | I Do |
| Survival | Success | Significance |

Unless you checked every entry in the middle column, you still have work to do when it comes to shifting your mindset from good intentions to intentional living.

For every entry where you checked the left column, write a sentence or two describing what you must do to embrace the attitude and demonstrate the actions of intentional living so that you get the results in the right column.

# I WANT TO MAKE
# A DIFFERENCE

# 3

## Start Small but Believe Big

My significance journey didn't truly begin until I decided I wanted to make a difference in the lives of others. I vividly remember the day that I became conscious of that desire. I was in the fourth grade and was walking across a campground with my father.

At that time Dad was an overseer of two hundred pastors in a very small denomination. Although he was in a leadership position over people, the position he had in their hearts superseded any formal position or authority he held. Dad was a constant encourager. He truly loved people and wanted to help them. On this particular day it took us thirty minutes to walk a hundred yards because people kept stopping Dad along the way. They were thanking Dad for kind things he had done for them and passing along thoughtful words.

I listened to the people speak so well of him, and even in those moments his focus was still on encouraging each and every person. I watched their faces as my dad talked to them, making his way across the grass, and I could see that he was lifting them higher than they could lift themselves. When I saw what that did for other people, I knew that I wanted to provide that same gift to people as well. I can remember thinking, *I want to be like my dad. I want to help people, too.*

This is where my desire to make a difference was birthed. As I reflect on that moment of realization, it provides clear evidence that you don't have to be a big person to have a big idea. After all, I wasn't anyone out of the ordinary. I was just a kid from southern Ohio. But something caught fire in my belly that day, and I inherently trusted that I had the capability to touch people's hearts in the same way my dad did. I hoped that if I believed in myself enough, others might be willing to believe in me, too. The only way I knew to do that was to follow in my dad's footsteps and enter the ministry. I wanted to lead with conviction, show kindness to others, and offer compassion wherever I went. I would study to become a pastor and be guided by the Golden Rule: Do unto others as you would have them do unto you.

While I considered myself to be an ordinary boy, I

recognize that my childhood was filled with extraordinary opportunities most children rarely receive. Because of my father's work, he had developed friendships with many noteworthy spiritual leaders from all over the world. So I was exposed to their teachings at a very young age. While I couldn't possibly appreciate the impact they would have on my life in those moments, I can surely look back now and recognize the effect they had on my path. Each one of these encounters left a lasting impression that shaped my life and my future toward intentionality and significance.

One of those important encounters happened when I was around twelve years old. My father took me to hear Norman Vincent Peale speak at the Veterans Memorial Auditorium in Columbus, Ohio. Dad was a big Peale fan. He was drawn to his messages about the power of a positive attitude. Dad had all of Peale's books in his library, and I had been encouraged to read them time and time again.

After hearing Peale speak, I immediately understood the attraction. I still remember walking down the wide concrete steps of Veterans Memorial Auditorium after that experience. My father turned to me and said, "Norman Vincent Peale is a great man, John, because he helps a lot of people."

By my teenage years, I was ready to tell my father

about my desire and intentions to follow his footsteps, to enter the ministry. The day I told my father how I felt, that I intended to enter the ministry, he put his arm around me and said, "That's wonderful, son." I could see that it touched his heart. He simply yet poignantly looked at me and asked, "What does that mean to you?"

"I am going to give my life to helping people."

He watched me closely, as if he was waiting to see if I would blink. Perhaps he was looking for signs that I might not be certain of my calling. But I had never been more committed to anything in my life. I didn't break our eye contact because I felt confident. This was what I was meant to do.

Dad smiled and said, "Then you are going to make a great difference, son."

I believe my father took tremendous pride in the idea that I would choose to honor him in such a way. And while it's true that he was my chief inspiration, the thought of helping others and having a positive impact on their lives was the engine that drove my passion the most.

As I drew closer toward my life's work, my father began to open more doors that helped me grow and continued to fire my desire to serve others. He introduced me to good leaders and took me to hear powerful speakers.

I will never forget the day Dad took me to hear the great E. Stanley Jones. To this day I consider it one of the most profound experiences of my life. As we drove to the event where Jones would speak, my father described him as one of the greatest missionaries and theologians who had ever lived. Though he was born in America, Jones had spent most of his life in India, where he started the Christian ashram movement. During this time, Jones had become a close friend of many prominent Indian families and leaders, including Mahatma Gandhi. After Gandhi's assassination, Jones wrote a biography of the Indian leader's life. (It was this book that inspired Martin Luther King Jr. to nonviolence in the civil rights movement.) To say that he was a powerful and inspirational figure would hardly be doing E. Stanley Jones justice.

At the end of Jones's talk that day, my father and I went off to a side room where we had the opportunity to meet the great missionary. He was a quiet man, not boisterous or grand in any way. I was taken by his gentleness.

He talked to my father for a short while. Toward the end of their conversation, my father explained that I really wanted to make a difference in people's lives. He asked E. Stanley Jones to pray over me, and this man who had lived such a significant life said he would be glad to.

I don't know why, but I was nervous. I could feel my heart pounding inside my chest. Jones laid hands on me—placing one hand on my shoulder and the other on my head—and in that instant, a sense of peace fell over me. I could feel it in every part of my body. My shoulders relaxed and I exhaled. I tried to soak in every aspect of the moment. I knew in my mind, body, and soul that this would leave a profound impact on me.

"God, empower this young man. Give him a heart for people and help him to be a person of compassion," he said. There was authority in his voice. His words still ring in my ears as I recall them.

Afterward, I knew without doubt that E. Stanley Jones had spoken that belief right into me. I left the room feeling much stronger, more self-assured and confident than I had when I walked in. And I felt three inches taller, too! I had been given a great gift. *I can change the world*, I thought. I had been shown a path—been pointed in a direction.

Later I thought about President Kennedy, who was in office at the time. I recalled his brave and powerful words: "Ask not what your country can do for you. Ask what you can do for your country." That speech greatly influenced my generation. Kennedy was an effective leader because he connected with people, especially the youth of the country. I was one of those kids who were inspired by him. So were my friends.

We were a nation ready for change, and for some of us, we believed we were the change.

*Why can't I be the one to make a difference?* I thought. It was as if I had been given a sign that said, "Your future → this way." It was my seminal moment. My fate, my path, my future was sealed.

Suddenly, the words of my fifth-grade teacher, Mr. Horton, came flooding back to me. Mr. Horton, whom I admired very much, had stopped me one day after recess and said, "John, you are a born leader. I've watched you on the playground at recess, and all of the other kids follow you. You are the one who determines what game everyone will play, who will be on your team, and what the outcome will be. You have excellent leadership skills, John. I think you will grow up to become a wonderful leader someday."

I've never forgotten his observation or what it meant to me. I had always seen my father as a wonderful inspirational leader, but Mr. Horton was the first person who ever articulated the idea of seeing leadership in me. That was the day I realized I might be a leader someday. And though at the time I didn't fully understand what that meant, it was a hint about my future. It would be almost twenty years later that I would understand how important leadership would be in my personal journey of significance, in how I would add value to people and make a difference.

## Be Willing to Start Small

I believe we all have a longing to be significant, to make a contribution, to be a part of something noble and purposeful. And to make that contribution, we need to be willing to focus on others. We need to give of ourselves. The action of intentionality I talked about in the previous chapter must be guided by the desire to improve the lives of others, to help them do what they perhaps cannot do by themselves. Are you with me?

Many people look at all that's wrong in the world and mistakenly believe that they cannot make a difference. The challenges loom large, and they feel small. And they think they must do big things to have a life that matters. Or they think they have to reach a certain place in life from which to do something significant.

Does that seed of doubt exist in you? Have you ever found yourself thinking or saying, "I will be able to make a difference only when . . .

I come up with a really big idea,
I get to a certain age,
I make enough money,
I reach a specific milestone in my career,

I'm famous, or
I retire"?

None of these things is necessary before you can start to achieve significance. You may not realize it, but those hesitations are really nothing more than excuses. The only thing you need to achieve significance is to be intentional about starting—no matter where you are, who you are, or what you have. Do you believe that? You can't make an impact sitting still. Former NFL coach Tony Dungy once told me, "Do the ordinary things better than anyone else and you will achieve excellence." The same is true for significance. Begin by doing ordinary things.

Chinese philosopher Lao Tzu said, "A journey of a thousand miles begins with a single step." That's true. In fact, so does every human being's *first* journey. As children, we had to learn how to take that first step in order to walk. We don't think anything of it now, but it was a big deal then.

*Every* big thing that's ever been done started with a first step. When Neil Armstrong took his first walk on the moon, he stated, "That's one small step for man, one giant leap for mankind." But the first steps of that achievement occurred decades before. We can't get anywhere in life without taking that first small step. Sometimes the step is hard; other times it's easy. But no matter what, you have to do it if you want to achieve big things.

You never know when something small that you do for others is going to expand into something big. That was true for Chris Kennedy, a golfer from Florida. In 2014, a friend nominated him to do the Ice Bucket Challenge for the charity of his choice. Kennedy passed along the challenge to his wife's cousin Jeanette Senercia because the two liked to tease and challenge each other. Kennedy chose amyotrophic lateral sclerosis (ALS) as his charity because Jeanette's husband suffered from the disease. Jeanette accepted the challenge, posted the video on her Facebook page, and nominated others.[5]

That was a small start of something big. In today's digital world we talk about things going viral. The term *viral* was coined because ideas and initiatives can spread quickly the way germs do. Almost anything that starts out as a single idea—a bold statement, a YouTube video, a creative or memorable photo—can gain vast popularity and quickly spread via the Internet.

The Ice Bucket Challenge soon went viral. If you somehow missed out on it, the idea was to either donate to the ALS Association or record a video of yourself being doused with ice water, and then challenge three other people to donate or get doused.

This turned out to be a brilliant idea to raise money to help fight a disease that many people otherwise might not have known about and would not have donated to. I participated in the challenge. Sure, I was aware of the disease, but it wasn't a charity I normally gave to. I was nominated by colleagues to take the challenge, and I was happy to participate.

Most people chose to give *and* get doused. When I accepted the challenge, I made a donation and asked three of my grandchildren to do the honors of soaking me. They used not one, but three, freezing cold buckets of water on me. Though I pleaded for compassion and warm water, the grandkids showed no mercy!

The best part is that over $113.3 million was donated between July and September of 2014 as a result of the Ice Bucket Challenge, compared to $2.7 million donated during the same period of time the previous year. On Facebook alone, over twenty-eight million people had uploaded, commented on, or liked Ice Bucket–related posts as of the last time I checked. The purpose of the campaign wasn't just to raise money. It was about raising awareness. But it accomplished both with great intentionality.

What can you do now? As you think about making a difference, be willing to start small. You never know whether your passion-fueled idea will have an outcome similar to that of the ALS Ice Bucket Challenge.

## My Small Start

My start in making a difference was surely small. It happened in June of 1969. In that month I graduated from college, married my high school sweetheart, Margaret, and accepted my first position as the pastor of a tiny church in rural Indiana, in a community called Hillham. The town had eleven houses, two garages, and one grocery store. Does that sound small enough?

I had high hopes and unlimited energy. I was ready to help people, so I jumped in. The first service I held in Hillham had three people in attendance. And two of them were Margaret and me!

I was not discouraged. I saw it as a challenge. I started doing what I could to help people in the community. I visited the sick, offered counseling, invited people to services, and taught messages to help people improve their lives. I did everything I knew how to do to add value to people.

As I look back now more than forty-five years later, I recognize some things that can help you and encourage you to start small but believe big:

## 1. Start Where You Are

Parker Palmer, a philosopher and author, wrote, "Our real freedom comes from being aware that we do not have to save the world, we must merely make a difference in the place where we live." That's what I tried to do. Hillham didn't look like much, but it was a great place to start the journey. It was in Hillham that I learned to value people, work hard, stay emotionally strong, solve problems, work well with others, and lead by example. It's where I took my first steps toward significance. In Hillham, in the poorest county in Indiana, while leading a congregation of conservative farmers who were far from wealthy, I became a person of abundance.

A pivotal experience at Hillham occurred just a few months after my arrival. Many of the people were struggling financially, so I sensed that they would benefit greatly from some teaching on stewardship, the management of our time and talents. Being young and inexperienced, I wanted to find some resources to help me develop my teachings. I remember going to a bookstore in Bedford, Indiana, to look for the help

I needed. For two hours I skimmed through dozens of books but found nothing written on this vital subject. Feelings of disappointment and panic filled my heart as I drove home empty-handed.

What was I going to do?

I had a sense of what I wanted to teach, but I didn't have the tools to communicate the lessons. When I shared my concerns with Margaret, we decided that if we couldn't find resources, we would create them ourselves.

We began by looking for quotes on stewardship, first in the Bible and then in other books. (Remember, this was way before Google.) After several days of reading and research, we had developed eight solid thoughts on the subject.

That evening we went into our garage and began painting poster boards different colors and writing the selected quotes on them. Eight posters later, we were ready to launch our first stewardship teaching. The next Sunday, we placed the freshly painted posters on the walls of our tiny church auditorium so that people could read them when they came to the service.

I laugh out loud every time I think about this. Why? Because my sermon had a lot more passion than content. But I engaged the crowd with my eagerness as I walked around the auditorium, stopping at each poster and exhorting them to embrace the ideas I explained. The posters looked, well, homemade with their childlike gaudy colors and unprofessional quality. And because of where we had placed them, people had to keep craning their necks to see them. You can bet everybody in the congregation was sore on Monday morning after having to look in every direction on that Sunday. The whole event was so basic, but the people talked about it for a long time in the most positive way.

Once people understood God's principles about money, they started to give generously to the church. And news about the people's faithful giving began to spread to other pastors in my denomination. They began asking me to share my program with them.

Shamefully, I did not want to do that. I felt that if I kept the methods I developed to myself, my church would grow past other churches, and my reputation would be elevated with that success. Even though I genuinely wanted to help people, I was also selfish and competitive. (I'll tell you more about this in chapter five.)

Sadly, for a couple of months I chose not share my approach with other pastors. Then one day my eyes were opened. I did the math. If I kept my ideas to myself, I would help a hundred people. If I shared them with other pastors, I could potentially help thousands. Being generous would make a greater impact. A few weeks later, I freely gave my entire stewardship program to others. And when I did, I experienced my first feelings of abundance—and yes, significance!

I felt good about myself. I was excited about what I had done for others. And most importantly, I felt that I would create more ideas because I had freely given away what I had to others instead of hoarding it for myself. It was at that moment that an image came to me that made it clear what God wanted me to be: a river, not a reservoir. Whatever I was given I was to allow to flow through me and pass on to others, not hold on to for myself. And I could do this because there would always be more. God would never run out.

Perhaps you are in a Hillham experience right now. You don't have much, and what little you do possess, you're holding on to for dear life. Let go. You don't need a lot to give. It's a matter of heart and attitude, not how much you have. Are you willing to give that a try? Mother Teresa said that some of the greatest works ever done have been performed from sick beds and in prison cells. Like her, you can be significant from wherever you are with whatever you have. Opportunity is always where you are. Be willing to start by giving of yourself.

## 2. Start with Your One Thing

I believe everybody has one thing they do better than anything else. The right place to start is with your one thing. I learned this from my dad. In fact it was a Maxwell house rule when I was growing up. When we were kids, my dad's message to my brother, sister, and me was to find your strength—your one thing—and stay with it. He never encouraged us to try to do lots of different things. He wanted each of us to do one thing exceptionally well. A long running joke in our family was that we felt sorry for multi-gifted people. How would they know which of their gifts to focus on?

In my eyes, my father became an exceptional man not because he was exceptionally gifted, but because he found his one thing and stuck with it. He was a great encourager. As a result, he rose to way above average. He mastered the art of encouraging others and never departed from it. Excellence comes from consistency in using our strengths, and Dad has been consistent.

Henry David Thoreau wrote, "One is not born into the world to do everything, but to do something." I found my something in Hillham: communication. That was what I focused on. I poured myself into it. I spent hours crafting my messages. I went to see good communicators every chance I got. I was determined to become the best I could.

I look back now and realize that back then my messages were very *informational*, but they weren't *transformational*. I wanted to facilitate transformation in others, but I was falling short. I didn't realize that I needed to change first. Viktor Frankl was right when he said, "When we are no longer able to change a situation, we are challenged to change ourselves." I'll talk about that change in the next chapter.

When I got started doing my one thing, I had no idea it would lead me to where I am today. Besides, even if I'd wanted to start big, I wasn't sophisticated enough to, so I just started with what I had and did it as well as I could. As a result, my ability multiplied. That came from working at it with consistency. I am where I am today, not because I have done several big things, but because I have worked at communicating ever since my twenties, and this intentionality has compounded in my life.

Investing in yourself is like taking a penny and doubling its value every day. If you did that for a month, how much would you end up with? A hundred dollars? A thousand dollars? A million dollars? Not even close.

If you start with just a single penny and double it every day for thirty-one days, you end up with $21,474,836.48. Personal growth is like that. Practice your one thing with excellence daily, and you will get a return. It's like putting money in the significance bank.

What's your one thing? What do you have the potential to do better than anything else? Do you have a sense of what that is? If not, then ask people who know you well. Or look at your history. Or take a personality or skills assessment to get clues. Don't think about what you can't do. Think about what you can. There is always a starting line. You just need to find it. It's about beginning with what you have, not with what you don't have. Find your one thing and start developing it.

## 3. Start Watching Your Words

Solomon, who was reputed to be the wisest man who ever lived, said, "Words kill, words give life; they're either poison or fruit—you choose."[6] If you want to make a difference and live a life that matters, you need to embrace some words and reject others. We all have a running dialogue in our heads. What we say to ourselves either encourages us or discourages us. The words we need to embrace are positive, words such as *we, can, will,* and *yes.* What do we need to eliminate? *Me, can't, won't,* and *no.*

During the season of my life when I was getting my start in Hillham, I realized there were words I had to reject if I wanted to make my life count in a positive way. I brainstormed a list of words that I believed were holding me back, and then went to my dictionary. As I found each negative word, I literally took a pair of scissors and cut it out. There was one word in particular that I hated: *quit*. I cut that word and every variation of it out of each of my four dictionaries.

My thesaurus wasn't safe either. When you're a public speaker, these books are like treasure troves. I used them often. But whenever I came across a page with a missing word, I was reminded of this symbolic act of positive thinking. It supported my intention to think positively and watch my words.

Perhaps you don't want to cut up your books. Maybe you don't even have a dictionary because you do your research online. Instead, you can try doing what my longtime friend Dianna Kokoszka does. Recently she told me about how she watches her words:

> I journal (wish I could say every day). I am very purposeful about writing in my journal, and once a month or so I scan what I have written and look for words that are used over and over again and write them down. Then I ask, "Are the words I use moving me towards being the person I choose to be? Are they words that I would love my family to use?"

Several years ago I saw the word *frustration* show up many times, so I changed it to fascination. No longer being frustrated, I began looking for opportunities where I could be fascinated with endless possibilities.

I also no longer choose to use the word *but* since that negates everything I have said before that word. I have eliminated *try*, too. As Yoda says, "There is no try."

*Yeah but* sends a message of an excuse or reason for not obtaining my goal, so I let that one go as well.

I wrote this as a law in bold in the course I teach: You can have reasons or results. You can't have both.

Words have power. Diana recognizes that and does something about it. No wonder she is such a positive person.

What kinds of words do you use—in your mind as you talk to yourself, out loud as you speak with others, and in your writing? Are they positive and encouraging? Do they encourage you to embrace a bigger vision? Or are they holding you back? Are they preventing you from doing small things that can ultimately make a big difference? Don't tell yourself that what you can do doesn't matter. It does.

## 4. Start by Making Small Changes

When Mother Teresa wanted to start her work in Calcutta, she was asked what she must do to consider the work successful. "I do not know what success will be," she replied, "but if the Missionaries of Charity have brought joy to one unhappy home—made one innocent child from the street keep pure for Jesus— one dying person die in peace with God—don't you think... it would be worthwhile offering everything for just that one?"

It's easy to forget that even someone who eventually did big things started out trying to make small changes. That's what I did in Hillham. I tried to make my sermons a little better each week. I tried to visit one more person who was sick. And I worked at shifting my time away from things I didn't do well, such as counseling, and putting more time and energy into things I did well, like communicating and leading.

Change can be difficult, but it becomes easier when you do it a little at a time. Nathaniel Branden, who is widely considered to be the father of the self-esteem movement, created what he called the 5 percent practice. He recommended trying to change 5 percent a day by asking yourself a question. For example, "If I were 5 percent more responsible today, what would I be able to do?"

This kind of thinking helps us to embrace incremental change. Trying to make a huge change overnight often creates fear, uncertainty, and resistance, because the change appears unachievable. The idea of making small changes is less threatening and helps us overcome our hesitation and procrastination. In fact, this is how Toyota transformed from a middle-of-the-pack automobile manufacturer to the largest in the world. Every person employed by the company is tasked with finding ways to make tiny improvements to every process Toyota performs. They understand that success is gained in inches at a time, not miles.

> **Success is gained in inches at a time, not miles.**

Give it a try. What can you improve by some small percentage? Can you find a way to organize your desk to be more efficient? Can you slightly rearrange your calendar to get more out of your day? Can you become just a bit better at the most important task you do for work? Can you read a book to broaden your thinking ever so slightly? Any small change that makes you better is worth making, because many small changes add up to major improvement over time.

## Believe Big

One of the most important steps you can take in life is to increase your belief. If you don't believe you can make a difference, guess what? You won't—no matter how talented you are, how many opportunities you receive, or how many resources you have at your fingertips. You have to believe.

That's one of the things I had going for me when I started out. Because my parents believed in me and loved me unconditionally, I was able to believe big.

## 1. I Believed in Myself

Throughout the years I've been a very lucky man who has been blessed to have many longtime friends. But the best friend I've ever had is *me*. I know that may sound strange. But as I already mentioned, we all talk to ourselves in our minds. We have a running dialogue. When I say I am my own best friend, I am really referring to self-belief. My belief in myself has encouraged me when no one else did. It has strengthened me when I had no other resources. Whether I was doing something significant or trivial, my belief in myself stayed with me when others didn't. The most important voice I listen to, the one I hear most often and I give the most weight to, is my own.

This belief in myself has kept me going when others doubted me or wanted to limit me. Here's what I mean:

- When I was twenty-five and many people thought I could not lead the largest church in my denomination, I thought I could—and I did.
- When I was twenty-seven and I told my wife I'd be a millionaire by the time I was forty, she thought I was nuts and worried she was in trouble! I wasn't nuts and she wasn't in trouble—and I accomplished that goal.
- When I said EQUIP, the nonprofit I founded with my brother in 1996, would train one million leaders around the world, some thought I was reaching too high, but I reached anyway—and it happened.
- When I had to make a thirteen-foot putt on the eighteenth hole at the AT&T Pebble Beach Pro-Am to make the cut and qualify for the final round, my caddy wasn't sure I could make it, but I was—and I did.

My belief in myself enables me to take first steps. You may be wondering, "Does your self-belief always have positive results?" My answer is no. But I experience more positive results because of my self-belief than I would if I was filled with self-doubt.

Do you believe in yourself? Your belief will drive your behavior. The thought *I don't think I can* often arises out of *I don't think I am*. You will never be more than how you see yourself. Steve Jobs said, "The people who are crazy enough to think they can change the world are usually the ones who do." I've seen many successful people whom others didn't believe in. But I've never met a successful person who didn't believe in him- or herself. Start believing in yourself and you will see a change in your ability to make a difference.

## 2. I Believed in My Mission

In 2004, I was interviewed by *New Man* magazine. They asked me to share my thoughts on knowing and embarking on life's mission. What I most remember about that interview was saying that our life's mission cannot be borrowed from someone else. It must be our own. Borrowed beliefs have no power, and a borrowed mission instills no conviction or passion for making a difference.

How do you discover your mission? By taking small steps. Too many times people make the mistake of thinking they can discover new experiences, ideas, or concepts without moving. They can't.

I've made my greatest discoveries in motion, especially traveling the world. I do my best thinking on the move—not sitting. You're supposed to leave footprints in the sands of time. Most people leave butt prints. You need to get moving. You need to experience new things. You cannot analyze what you don't know. However, the moment you discover something new, your thinking goes to a deeper level.

I am not sure everyone has a mission. I am not even certain everyone has a dream. I used to think everyone did, but now I am not so sure. What I do know is, even people who don't have a dream can connect with someone who does. I believe that's what makes a great cause great. People identify with its goal and want to be a part of it. Just because you aren't leading a mission doesn't mean you don't have a purpose. If you don't feel you have a compelling mission, you can buy into somebody else's cause, make it your own, and still make a difference. You've got to find something that stirs you, even if it's not a mission that started within yourself. It can be a mission that comes from outside you as long as it's something that you buy into completely and participate in with passion.

In Hillham, my mission began by helping people. Since then it has grown and evolved. Every time I learn and grow, so does my mission. I didn't need the whole picture early in my journey, and neither do you. Act on your feelings of compassion. Go with your desire to make a difference. Are you willing to do that? Peter Senge says, "Mission instills the passion and the patience for the long journey." It also gives the impetus to get started.

### 3. I Believed in My People

I told you that I started my career in Hillham. What I haven't told you is that I could have chosen to go to a different church. It looked like a better opportunity. The church was larger. It had more money. It was in a more prestigious community. They would have accepted me as their pastor because of my father's good reputation. But I wanted to earn my own way. My father agreed that choosing the smaller rural church would be good for me. And he was right.

The people of Hillham were mostly farmers. They were solid people who lived straightforward lives. They worked hard. They had faith. They cared about one another. I quickly came to love them. And that is important. You can't really do anything for others if you don't care for them. I believed in them and wanted the best for them. And they knew it.

When you work with a person who truly believes in you, don't you respond to them based on their level of belief in you? Don't you perform better for a boss you want to please, or for a teacher who encourages you, or for a coach who inspires you? You work harder because of that belief factor.

As you get started in your small efforts to make a difference, work with people you believe in, people you care about. Or better yet, begin to care about and believe in the people who are already in your life. It will give you the desire to do things for them, to make a difference in their lives.

## 4. I Believed in My God

I've already told you that I don't want to force my faith on you or offend you. So if my talk about God bothers you, skip ahead to the next section. But I can't be true to myself and tell you my whole story without telling you how I feel about God.

It is always my desire to do my best. I have adopted Coach Wooden's motto "Make every day your masterpiece," so it's a given that I will give my best every day. But God helps to make my best, as flawed as it is, even better. I have always believed that God will be there for me and help me. In fact, my belief in myself grows out of my faith. I totally embrace the words in Jeremiah 29:11: "'For I know the plans I have for you,' declares the Lord, 'plans to prosper you and not to harm you, plans to give you hope and a future.'"[7] That has given me confidence to act, and if you also embrace faith, it will give you confidence, too.

Faith permeates every aspect of my life, and that of course includes my interaction with my grandkids. Because Margaret and I desire to create great memories for them, every year our Christmas gift to our family is a trip. For Christmas in 2014, we took our children and grandchildren to Hawaii. Before the trip, Margaret and I selected a Scripture verse, found a quote, and wrote a three-sentence prayer for each grandchild. When we were in Hawaii, we sat with each of the five of them and shared these things with them. The verse we picked for our oldest granddaughter, Maddie, was "I can do all things through Christ who strengthens me."[8] The quote we chose to accompany that verse was based on a quote by Catherine Bramwell-Booth: "Anybody can do their best. God helps us do better than our best."

Bob Pierce, the founder of World Vision, called this "God room." It was the gap between what he could humanly accomplish and what could happen only if God helped him. I have chosen to leave a lot of "God room" in my life also. I firmly believe God will make up the difference if my heart is right and I do my best. The verse in the Bible that best describes this "God room" is Ephesians 3:20, which says, "God can do anything, you know—far more than you could ever imagine or guess or request in your wildest dreams! He does it by working within us."[9]

There is only one thing in my life that I value more highly than intentional living in order to achieve significance, and that is God. He can do more than I can imagine, guess, or dream about. I always want Him as my partner. I feel like one little fellow who knelt at the side of his bed, closed his eyes, and prayed, "God bless Mom. God bless Dad. God bless Grandma." He said it the same way every time. But one night he added, "And please take care of yourself, God. 'Cause if anything happens to you, we're all sunk!"

## It Started with a Small Idea

I hope the story of how I got my start is an encouragement to you. I truly believe that everyone can make a difference if they're willing to take small steps. And I was again reminded of how true and powerful small ideas can be not long ago when I met a young woman named Carrie Rich. In December of 2013, she told me an incredible story.

Though only in her twenties, she was working as a senior director for Inova Health System in Virginia, and one day she got an idea. She wanted to do something positive for others, and she thought that with a small amount of money, she could get others to contribute to organizations that were already making a difference.

She was excited about the idea, so she told her boss, Knox, who had been the CEO of Inova for thirty years. His response was, "That's nice, Carrie, but could you go back to work now?" But then two months later for her birthday, he gave her a card. In it were two things—$100 and a quote attributed to John Wesley: "Do all the good you can. By all the means you can. In all the ways you can. In all the places you can. At all the times you can. To all the people you can. As long as ever you can."

Carrie says that Knox had taken some "lunch money"—the money he would have spent on her birthday lunch—and given it to her to put to good use. So what would she do?

She decided that she would try to turn the $100 into $1,000 for each of six organizations. In today's world where Bill and Melinda Gates have given away $28 billion, that amount probably sounds small. But that didn't discourage Carrie. She wrote to organizations in Washington, DC, Haiti, Tanzania, and elsewhere to ask what they would do with $1,000. The DC-area organization said it could improve literacy rates for a class of students. The Haitian organization said it could sustain ten families by using community agriculture. The Tanzanian organization could send twenty-five women through secondary school.

These stories ignited Carrie's passion. She was ready to act. But how? How could she turn $100 into $6,000? She decided to do something she had never done before. She wrote individual e-mail requests to family and friends—ultimately to every name that came up from her contacts list as she typed alphabetically in the "To" field. She even decided to write to the names that popped up that she didn't recognize. As she came to the "Subject" field, she wondered what to write. When she could come up with nothing better, she wrote, "The Global Good Fund."

It wasn't long before money started coming in: $20, $50, $1,000. "It was extraordinarily generous," says Carrie, "particularly from my peers who were just starting in the workplace. It really resonated with them."

Within two weeks, Carrie had received $6,052. She felt good. She had started small, but she had accomplished her goal. She was ready to give the money to the six organizations. *All done!* she thought. Little could she guess what would happen next.

As the donations were coming in, she had also received an e-mail from someone she had met for five minutes at a conference the year earlier. They had exchanged cards that day, and Carrie had sent him a "nice to meet you" e-mail afterward. That's why his name had been in her contacts. The return e-mail from the man, who wanted to remain anonymous, said, "I'd like to donate a million dollars to the Global Good Fund. Where should I send the check?"

Carrie's reaction: "This guy's pranking me. I'm not giving him my home address!"

She e-mailed him back saying that if he was serious, he was to meet her on a particular day at a specific time in a specific place (a very public one with security cameras). And she would wait only ten minutes.

When he arrived, he handed her a bank-certified check for $1 million, made out to "The Global Good Fund," an organization that did not exist. And his question for Carrie was the same one she had asked the six organizations: What will you do with this money?

Carrie had not prepared for such a question because, honestly, she didn't think the guy would show up. She couldn't fathom someone she'd met for five minutes doing that. She quickly thought about what had made a difference in her life, and she told him she would invest in young leaders around the world who were using entrepreneurship for social impact. As others had invested in her, she would help these leaders to grow personally so that they could be a gift to society. He handed her the check.

Not knowing what to do, Carrie went back to her office and asked to see her boss, Knox. His assistant,

Carol, could see that Carrie was sweating and hyper-ventilating, so she escorted her right in.

"Look what you've done," she said, slamming the check down on his desk. "You gave me the lunch money, and this stranger gave me a million dollars for an organization that doesn't even exist! I have no idea what to do with the money. Would you please help me?"

"I'll help you under two conditions," said Knox. "First, while you may report to me at work, I'd like to report to you at the Global Good Fund. Second, I'm going to match the initial gift."

Carrie says, "You know that expression 'You fell out of your chair'? I literally fell. Carol came in and she helped me back up. And that's how it started."

That was in 2011. A year later, she stopped working for Inova and became the CEO of the Global Good Fund, which she created as a nonprofit organization. She has begun a fellowship program and is already investing in nineteen young leaders in countries around the world. And she continues to seek opportunities to make a difference.

How big will the Global Good Fund become? How great an impact will it make? I don't know. Carrie is still young. But does it matter? She is making a difference now. She is helping people and making the world a better place for her having been in it. And isn't that what matters?

## Intentional Application: Start Small but Believe Big

Most people want to believe big and start big, or believe small and start small. It goes against the grain to believe as big as you can and be willing to take very small steps. Yet that's what 99 percent of people must do to make a difference.

### What Do You Believe?

Believing big begins with believing in yourself. Do you believe you can make a difference? Do you believe you have a contribution to make that can positively impact the world? Or are your beliefs about yourself holding you back?

Test it. Take some time to write out all the positive things you can think of about yourself. What do you bring to the table of life? I challenge you to write twenty, fifty, or even one hundred positive things about yourself.

### Your One Thing

After you brainstorm and write down the positive potential you bring to this world, take a look at your list. What is your one thing? What is the thing you do better than anything else you do? The authors of *StrengthsFinder 2.0* say that every person does something better than the next ten thousand people.

What's yours? You may be able to name it instantly, instinctively. If so, great. I hope you're already developing that strength for all it's worth. If not, one of the tasks I encourage you to do before you finish reading this book is to figure out what it is. Look at your personal history. Question your friends and family. Talk to your colleagues. Ask your boss. Take aptitude tests. Do whatever it takes. Until you identify and tap into your one thing, you may find your life going around in circles, and significance will be elusive.

## You Are Here!

One of the reasons people don't start small is that they can see a better starting place than where they are. *If I could just be there*, they think, *then starting would be easier.* But the only place anyone can start is where he or she is. I started in Hillham because that's where I was. If I had waited until I was somewhere else, somewhere better, I never would have done anything worthwhile.

Define where you are and what you have right now. Carrie Rich had a desire to make a difference, lunch money, and an e-mail list. What do you have? Take an inventory. Look at your opportunities. Think about where you currently are. Figure out what's working for and against you. Get the process started.

In the next chapter, I'll prompt you to go deeper inside and tap into what really matters to you. But in the meantime, you need to be willing to get started.

# 4

## Search Until You Find Your *Why*

When I started my career in Hillham in 1969, the model I had in my mind for helping people was the traditional picture of a shepherd. That's how pastors were trained back then. The emphasis was on feeding and caring for the flock, protecting them and keeping them together. That matched my heart for the people of Hillham, whom I immediately fell in love with in that wonderful community. But I soon discovered that image didn't fit my gifts and temperament. I was not a natural shepherd. I was more of a *rancher.*

What do I mean by that? I cared *about* people, but I was not content to merely care *for* people. I didn't get excited about sitting around the campfire with existing members and singing "Kumbaya." My real passion was to reach new people and invite them to join

111

us. I wanted to march onward with Christian soldiers and take new territory. I wanted to build something. I wanted to be a pioneer and a leader.

That quickly prompted me to begin asking myself some soul-searching questions that I hadn't expected so soon in my career.

Was I doing something wrong?

Should I change?

Did I miss my calling?

During this time of questioning, I read a book called *Spiritual Leadership* by J. Oswald Sanders. In this book, Sanders writes about the need for vigorous, talented leaders in the church and presents the key principles of leadership in both the earthly and spiritual realms. He illustrates his points with examples from Scripture and the biographies of other eminent men of God, such as David Livingstone and Charles Spurgeon.

The message of the book was another eureka moment for me in my journey of significance because I suddenly realized my gifting called me to become a leader—someone who innovates and takes new ground—rather than a pastor who cares for people. This began a shift in my thinking that played out a few years later in my next position. But in the meantime, I started to look at myself and my calling differently. My thinking was starting to change, and my horizons were starting to expand. Something was stirring within me. It was making me think more about what I was doing, and more important, *why.*

## Inspiration

Then something happened on a Sunday morning. Someone came into our church in Hillham holding a bulletin with the picture of a church he'd been to in Hammond, Indiana.

"I went to services here last week," the man said excitedly. "They've got four thousand people in their congregation!"

Wow! I could hardly fathom that. In college, when I had been encouraged to set some goals, I dreamed of someday, by the end of my career, having a church of five hundred people. It was as big as I could imagine. Now I was hearing about a church eight times the size of that. It struck a chord deep within me. It challenged and inspired me.

"Can I have that bulletin?" I asked.

He gave me the bulletin, and I taped it to a folder that I carried around with me every day for the next several years. Whenever I looked at it, I'd say to myself, "I can do this. I am going to build one of the largest churches in America. I will do this." Several times a day, every single day, I fed my mind, body, and spirit with the belief that I had the power and capacity to turn that dream into a reality.

If you had known me then, you probably would have shaken your head and thought I was disconnected from reality. My church was tiny. I had only a couple of years of experience, and the largest church in my area had 570 people. No one around me believed I could build a large church. But I was convinced it was possible. How could I have such confidence? I was beginning to tap into my *why*.

## Why Your *Why* Is Important

Later in this chapter, I'll tell you how tapping into my *why* played out for me in Hillham. But first I want to stop and talk to you about your *why*. If you want to make a difference and live a life of significance, you must tap into your *why*. You need to start thinking about your purpose. I'm certain everybody has one. Your *why* is the life's blood of intentional living.

If you know your *why* and focus on going there with fierce determination, you can make sense of everything on your journey because you see it through the lens of *why*. This makes the way so much more meaningful and complete because you have context to understand the reason you're on the journey in the first place.

Recently while speaking to a group on the subject of purpose, I made the following statement: "Once you find your *why*, you will be able to find your *way*." How do those things differ? *Why* is your purpose. *Way* is your path. When you find your *why*, your path automatically has purpose.

During the Q&A that followed, someone asked, "Does the *why* always have to come first? Can you find your way and then find your *why*?"

You may be wondering the same thing. What has to come first? The good news is that either can be first. But if the *why* comes before the *way*, your ability to make a difference will come more quickly and immediately be more effective.

Think of it like this. Have you ever wondered why people often find great joy in packing for a vacation? They spend weeks building up great anticipation, looking forward to those warm days on a tropical beach or trips down the slopes of their favorite ski resort. So they pick out each item that goes into the suitcase with great purpose.

> **If the *why* comes before the *way*, your ability to make a difference will come more quickly and immediately be more effective.**

When you get ready for a trip, almost all of your

effort is focused on the purpose of the trip. That's why it's a lot more fun to pack for a trip than it is to unpack afterward. This concept applies more broadly to our lives. Whatever path you travel, you're going to be able to do things more significantly because you understand your purpose for being there.

When you start your day with your *why,* you will find yourself continually doing things that inspire you. That is certainly true for me. Finding my *why* gave me the focused and driven energy that I still feel today.

I'm convinced that most people want to live a life of purpose. The vast popularity of Rick Warren's book *The Purpose Driven Life* was in part based on this desire, which became evident when millions of people bought the book. Rick writes, "Humans were made to have meaning. Without purpose, life is meaningless. A meaningless life is a life without hope or significance. This is a profound statement and one that everyone should spend time pondering. God gives purpose. Purpose gives meaning. Meaning gives hope and significance. There is awesome truth contained within that logic."

> "Humans were made to have meaning. Without purpose, life is meaningless. A meaningless life is a life without hope or significance."
>
> —*Rick Warren*

Just think of the difference knowing this message would make to a young person just starting his or her life. When I read Rick's book, it was an affirmation of how I have lived. I got so excited about it that I wanted to buy it and give it to every twenty-year-old I knew. Purpose empowers significance.

## How Your *Why* Helps You Find Your Way

If you tap into your *why*, as I did, your life will open up to significance. It will be within your reach every day because you will be able to do simple things that matter. Significance is usually not a result of anything spectacular. It's based on small steps in line with purpose. Knowing your *why* helps you to know what to do and to follow through. Here's how:

### 1. Knowing Your *Why* Allows You to Focus More on Others and Less on Yourself

Purpose comes from within. It works from the inside out. What happens when you don't know your *why*? You have to spend a lot of time looking within yourself to find it, and trying new things to see what fits you and what doesn't. There's nothing wrong with that. How else will you know what's important to you? But it takes time. It requires effort. You need to ask yourself lots of questions. And all the while, your focus will be on yourself.

> The sooner you know your why, the sooner you can shift your focus from yourself to others.

The sooner you know your *why*, the sooner you can shift your focus from yourself to others. The sooner you can just get on with it. You can lose yourself in others. That is where significance lives and thrives.

We all have to find ourselves before we can lose ourselves. If you are preoccupied with trying to understand your personality, identify your talents, and learn the basics in your skill set, it's hard to think about others. Know yourself and settle your *why*, and you'll have the capacity to focus on others.

## 2. Living Out Your *Why* Gives You a Confidence That Is Attractive to Others

Knowing my *why* gives me great security and comfort in everything I attempt and do. That confidence and self-assuredness is usually appealing and reassuring to others, because most people long for it.

Have you ever noticed people who walked into a room and you could feel their presence? They just seemed to know what they were doing and where they were going. They brought energy into the room. It's almost like their presence entered the room before they did. That's not ego or arrogance. It's *purpose*. People with purpose walk with an air of distinction, as if they have a *why* in every step. Wouldn't you like to have that same sense of purpose?

Purpose is the rudder on your boat. It gives you direction and keeps you going in the right direction when the wind is blowing and the waves are crashing against you. It provides calm and confidence in the midst of a storm. People who know their *why* can keep their heads while everything around them is in turmoil. And that draws others to them.

## 3. The More You Live Your *Why,* the More You Layer It

People's strengths and their individual purposes are always connected. I embrace that truth because I believe God has gifted everyone with the ability to be great at what they are supposed to do. But you don't have to be a person of faith to make the connection between talent and purpose. Your *why* is fuel for your strengths. And your strengths are the *way* to fulfill your *why*.

Every time you use your strengths to live out your *why,* you build on your strength and increase your *why*. Living this way adds layers of ability, purpose, credibility, and significance to your life. The more you do, the more you learn, because you are layering each experience into your life.

Think about it like this. When you start off doing something, you are usually not very good at it. But with time and practice, you get better. After a while, you create layers of success that you can build on, and you also build up tremendous confidence as a result. That's what great athletes do. They don't start off playing their sport at a professional level. It takes years of practice to get to the highest level. How do they do it? They layer wins, losses, pain, and gain.

As I write this, I am looking at the Canadian Rockies. When I look up at the majestic mountains, I am always in awe of their rugged stature and endless beauty. I am aware that every cut I see in the rock is a record of history for that mountain. Each jagged edge tells a story. Thousands, if not millions, of years of sand, soil, and minerals impacted by heat, water, wind, and rain have formed the statuesque vision I see when I gaze out my hotel window. The horizontal layers show the natural changes that have occurred over time. The layers reflect the formation of that mountain. When you know your *why*, you know the history and purpose of each experience in your life.

## 4. The More You Layer Your *Why*, the More Impact It Has on Others

Purpose is like a snowball rolling downhill—it builds over time. It compounds. Doing the right thing for the right reason with the right people—over time—gives you a huge significance return, and ultimately a giant significance reputation. Why do I say that? Because I've experienced it. I've given

> **Purpose is like a snowball rolling downhill—it builds over time.**

my life to helping others, and because I've stuck with it, people recognize me for it.

Most people want to see a high return on their efforts right way. They want to be given reputation credit in advance. That's not how life works. You have to earn credibility. Keep acting according to your purpose and doing significant acts day by day, year by year, decade after decade, and your impact will keep increasing. Will you be able to see that increase every day? Maybe not. But it will be there. And remember: a day of significant living may be delightful, but a lifetime of significant living can be magnificent.

## 5. Knowing Your *Why* Keeps You in the Game Longer

Have you ever known someone who died soon after retiring? I have. Why does it happen? Because people have a harder time living without a *why* to live for. What incentive do people have to keep living when there is no purpose for their actions, no reason to get out of bed each morning?

I don't ever want to retire. I'm like my dad. I want to keep living and giving until I've got nothing left. To this day, my dad's still in the game, and he is ninety-four years old! Every morning he gets up excited. Why? Because he still has his *why*! Every day he visits old people—it never dawns on him that he *is* an old person. Everyone he meets is someone whom he wants to encourage to keep going, to keep focusing on their reasons to live. He makes fifty pastoral visits a week to various homes.

People who know my dad say to me, "You're blessed to have his genes." I agree. But I'm even more blessed to know my *why*. That will sustain me a long time. I'm going to live fully until I die. And God willing, I've still got a long way to go. But when I finally do pass and I am six feet in the ground, I hope they put on my epitaph, "Here lies a man who lived with purpose and intentionality," because that's how I want to be remembered.

Do you know your *why*? Finding it is usually a process. You probably won't do it overnight, and you won't get the whole thing at once. It comes bit by bit as you take steps forward. That's why it's so important to start small—and it's why I discussed the idea of starting small but believing big in the last chapter, before introducing the idea of finding your *why*. It's almost a catch-22. To find your *why*, you need to take steps forward while believing. But to take steps forward and believe, you need to find your *why*. So which do you do first? Whichever one you can. Do the thing you're best positioned to do.

## Breaking through a Barrier

Back when I was at Hillham, I was doing these things at the same time. I was believing that I could someday build a large church, I was starting to figure out my *why*, and I was taking small steps of significance. One of those steps—which was actually a big step for me—was identifying a day when we would invite a record number of people to the church.

As I already mentioned, when I arrived at the

church, not a lot of people attended regular services. The church had gone through a split before
my arrival, and the few people who did attend didn't
have a lot of confidence in themselves or the church.
However, I was young and energetic, and soon people started coming. Within a year, a hundred people
were coming to services on a regular basis.

My big step was to announce on a Sunday in July
that on the first Sunday in October, we would have a
special day of celebration. I boldly set the goal of having three hundred people in attendance that day.

This audacious goal, which was a natural out-
growth of my emerging purpose, collided with the
low expectations and poor self-image of many of the
people who attended on a regular basis. To say they
had doubts would be putting it mildly.

"Is this goal possible?" they asked.

"Where will we get all of the people?"

"Where will we *put* them?"

"How in the world can we do this?"

It looked impossible to them. But for every objec-
tion and each potential problem they presented, I
responded with a positive answer. And I did my best
to lead them well. I won't say they got on board right
away, but they at least were willing to give it a chance.

As the word got out about what we were trying,
people started getting curious about the church. And

they started coming. Attendance grew every week. As it did, I could see the tide slowly changing, and it filled my heart with joy because I knew it had the potential to help people. Soon members of the congregation gained confidence and started inviting friends. Then their friends brought others. We had started small, but our little church was slowly growing with every passing week. And anticipation began to replace hesitation as the church filled.

So maybe I wasn't a typical pastor. Maybe my *why* was a little bit different from those of my former college classmates and my colleagues. But one thing was certain. I was seeing new people come into the church.

Finally, the big day in October arrived. As I looked over the crowd, it seemed as if the entire village was in attendance. Our tiny sanctuary was overflowing with people. We filled the basement with people, too. And we even wired a home beside the church with sound and filled it with people. If we could have figured out how to put them on the roof, we'd have done it!

To say the people were excited is a gross understatement. The feeling in the church was electric. Right before I was to preach, our lay leader stood up and happily announced our attendance for the day: 299 people. Everybody cheered.

Except me.

"What was our attendance goal?" I asked.

"Three hundred," they shouted with enthusiasm.

"We are one short, and I am not speaking until we reach our goal," I declared.

As a very young, confident leader, I pronounced that I would go out and find that one person and bring him or her to church. And *only* then would I preach.

I wasn't being defiant so much as determined. I was committed to reaching this goal no matter what it took.

As I walked down the aisle toward the door, several people stood up and patted me on the back, offering kind words of encouragement as I headed out the door. "Go get 'em, pastor."

I was pumped—until I stood outside. Alone.

*Now what am I going to do?* I thought.

I had no plan to speak of. "Think John, think," I said to myself. And then, it dawned on me.

Across the street from our church stood an old service station, owned by Sandy Burton. I looked over and spied Sandy and Glenn Harris sitting right out front.

I saw hope.

"Preacher, did you hit your goal?" Sandy asked as I walked across the street.

"Not yet," I said. "We are one short."

Sandy smiled.

"Which one of you would like to be the hero to all of those people inside that church by helping us achieve our goal?" I asked.

They looked at each other and said, "We both want to be the hero!"

Sandy closed up his station and both men walked with me across the road.

I dramatically flung open the door to the church with not one, but *two* people by my side.

The folks inside could not contain their joy. They stood to their feet, clapped, and cheered as if I had brought two heroic sons home from war. They slapped our backs and shook our hands all the way up the aisle. I moved two members off the front row and sat Sandy and Glenn there, as they were our guests of honor.

When everyone was settled, I moved to the pulpit and announced in a low calm tone that we had indeed reached our goal—plus one. We had 301 people in church with us that day.

After the service, all 301 of us stood in front of that old country church and took a photograph to commemorate our collective triumphant moment. It was a glorious day, one I've always treasured. Through the years I have had my picture taken at all sorts of significant events around the world and with many important people, but that picture of us standing jubilantly in front of our church is by far my absolute favorite.

Why?

Because that was the first big tangible expression of my *why*: using leadership to add value to people.

That day I became a leader in the eyes of my people. I put a win under their belt. I helped them gain confidence. I helped them gain victory. And in the process I experienced the joy of successfully leading others in something big for the very first time.

I had found my niche. I would make a difference by being a leader. This was the path of significance for me. And I must say, in all my years of leadership, I have never lost that thrill of helping people achieve something big that benefitted them.

Leading people has been at the center of my *why* ever since that day in Hillham. And it has continued to grow. It has led me to many places I never dreamed I could reach. It took me to Lancaster, Ohio, where I would lead a new congregation in another church. And it took me to Skyline Church in San Diego. I'll tell you more about that later, but for now I will say this. That dream I had in the early 1970s of building a large, influential church came true more than a decade later when Skyline became one of the twenty most influential churches in America. My *why* helped me find my *way*, and it accelerated my steps forward in significance.

## Everyone Has a *Why*

I believe every person has a *why* and has the ability to find it. Do you believe that too? If not, are you willing to accept the idea? If you haven't already found yours, I believe you can. Why am I convinced of that?

Every person was created to do his or her part to better mankind. That includes you!

Every person has talents that will help him or her better mankind. That includes you!

Every person is given an opportunity to better mankind. That includes you!

Every person has a purpose for which he or she was created. That includes you!

Every person must look within to discover his or her purpose. That includes you!

Some people seem to be born having a sense of their *why*. I believe Dolly Parton is one of those people. Margaret has been a longtime fan of hers, and not long ago she handed me an article from *Guideposts* magazine about Dolly. From the time she was a child, she knew what she was meant to do. In the article Dolly says,

> I'd put a tin can on a stick for a microphone, jab one end into a crack in the porch of our cabin, and sing a song that I'd made up.
>
> All at once those weren't our chickens listening to me out there in the yard. They were an audience full of people clapping and cheering. And that wasn't a hand-me-down shift I was wearing; it was a silk dress aglitter with rhinestones.
>
> Mama's people were all musical. "Sing one of your songs," she'd say, and I'd sing. My uncle Louis saw how serious I was about music, so he gave me a guitar, a baby Martin. Oh, I loved that guitar! I played it all the time.[10]

Dolly sang at every opportunity she got, and performed on the radio when she was just a kid. As a young woman, she went to Nashville to try to make it in music, and her talent was quickly recognized. She soon began performing with Porter Wagoner.

Her *why* was fueled when one of Wagoner's musicians gave her a book for her birthday. It was *The Power of Positive Thinking* by Norman Vincent Peale.

"He knew how to talk to a country girl like me...

'Dream big, think big, pray big,'" she says. "*Lord,* I thought, *that's just what I want to spend my life doing!*"

Maybe you already have a strong sense of your *why*, just as Dolly Parton does. If so, you already have a great head start on your significance journey. However, if you're like most people, you would be grateful to have some help figuring out your *why*. I want to help you with that.

The process begins with questions. I love to ask questions. They have unlocked more doors of opportunity for me than anything else I have ever done. So I ask questions in any and every kind of situation. And then I listen to the answers. That's where learning begins to happen.

My mother is the one who taught this to me. It seemed she always had time for me. Always. And whenever she gave her time to me, I knew I had her full attention. We would sit down together and she would listen to me, sometimes for hours. She always listened until I was talked out. No interruptions, with continual visual expressions to let me know that she was hearing every word and understanding the feelings that accompanied each idea. She heard with her ears and connected with her eyes. Her heart constantly gave me unconditional love.

Does it sound like she was a saint? She was. She was my mother!

Mom asked questions only when I was finished talking. They were filled with amazing insight because she always heard me out. Her reflective nature allowed her to think through each question she asked and couch it in a context of love. Her questions helped me sort out my feelings and caused me to reflect. It was at her side that I learned to listen and ask questions. My mother passed away in 2009, and I miss her greatly.

The first question you must ask yourself is this: How can I add value to others? If you can quiet yourself enough to listen for that answer from within yourself, you will begin to understand your *why*. I have to tell you that *this question has been the foundation and driver of every significant act in my life.* Did you get that? Having a life that matters comes from the ability to add value to others. This is where significance starts. Let that idea stir within you while I show you more specifically how to find your *why*.

> The first question you must ask yourself is this: How can I add value to others?

## Three Clues to Your *Why*

Back in 1965, when I was studying for my bachelor's degree at Ohio Christian University, a speaker came to my Psychology 101 class and asked us three questions. To this day, these questions have shaped my life. At the time, I was only an eighteen-year-old freshman, and I was not sure of my answers. But the questions stayed with me, and I have revisited them again and again over the years. I'll share them with you now, because I believe they will help you find and better understand your *why*.

## Question 1: What Do You Cry About?

This first question asks you to look inside yourself and think about what breaks your heart. What disturbs you? What inflicts emotional pain? What causes you so much discomfort that you are motivated to take action and do something to bring healing to that situation?

When I heard this question at eighteen, I didn't have a clear answer. Today, I do. My heart breaks when I see people falling short of who they could be. People have so much potential, and many fall short and live broken and unfulfilled lives. It brings tears to my eyes.

Because I have gifts and talents in the areas of communication and leadership, I feel a great sense of responsibility to try to help people in this area, to inspire and lead them to change and grow to their potential. I feel the weight of it on my shoulders every day. What does carrying that weight mean to me?

First, it means I am always conscious of my calling to help others find significance in their lives. When I see people, I see their greatest potential. I see them as potential "tens." My overwhelming desire is that they see it, too. I want them to shake off the mental and emotional shackles that bind them and run the race of life with excellence and exuberance. And any time I can help someone do that, it raises my spirits and makes me think, *I was born for this!*

Recently I had a lunch with three wonderful people: Michael D'Adamo, the CEO of T.O.P. Marketing Group, and his friends Jon and Laura-Ashley Manning. I was humbled when Jon said that having lunch with me had been on his bucket list. The four of us had a great time telling stories and exchanging leadership experiences.

At one point in our conversation, Michael bravely and openly shared about his heartbreaking childhood. After dropping out of school in ninth grade, he spent his time smoking dope and chasing women. To use his own words, he was "a bum." Michael said that based on their early years, neither he nor Jon would have been identified by anyone who knew them as a person who would make a difference in the lives of others, yet both of these men are now helping thousands of people.

What was the genesis of their turnarounds? Remarkably, they said it was reading my book *The 21 Irrefutable*

*Laws of Leadership.* Both say it caused them to see themselves differently. "As I read," Jon said, "I felt your belief pour into me with every turn of the page."

Michael added, "I began to see myself as a person of value. And that changed the way I started seeing others."

As I sat at the table listening to these two incredibly accomplished businessmen share their stories and discoveries, I was humbled. I wrote the book to help people, but to actually hear someone explain how it had helped him realize his God-given potential was extremely rewarding. Such experiences make the weight of responsibility for helping others feel just a bit lighter.

The second thing I understand about the weight I am carrying is that I must be a voice that calls people to intentional living. And I use the word *call* purposely because for me, it is a calling. I need to give expression to people's longing to make a difference and let them know that it is within their reach. Perhaps that's why I identify with the words of Elizabeth Rundle Charles, who wrote in the *Chronicles of the Schonberg-Cotta Family*, "To know how to say what other people only think, is what makes men poets and sages; and to dare to say what others only dare to think, makes men martyrs or reformers."

The third thing the weight of this calling means to me is that I believe I am supposed to be a catalyst in bringing people together to do significant works.

Leadership is my life; I get an enormous charge from casting vision and then bringing people together to reach a level of significance that is impossible without a team effort. It is at the core of my *why*.

So, what makes you cry? What makes your heart break? What touches you at the depths of your soul? Do you already know the answer? Or is it something you need to start exploring and thinking about?

When trying to figure out what makes you cry, you can look at your personal history. You can think back to your childhood. You can tap into social justice issues that get you angry. You can think about the last thing you got highly emotional about—or the thing that you *always* get emotional about. Any of these things can be clues to what makes you tick. And they will help you identify your *why*.

## Question 2: What Do You Sing About?

What always makes you happy? What puts a bounce in your step? What makes you jump for joy or spontaneously break into song? Back when I first heard this question, my answers didn't have a lot of depth: good grades, friends, food, and sports. What do you expect? I was only eighteen.

Today, nothing makes me happier than seeing people become intentional about making a difference. I believe this is the key to transforming our world. Poet Ralph Waldo Emerson said, "The purpose of life is not to be happy. It is to be useful, to be honorable, to be compassionate, to have it make some difference that you have lived and lived well." I believe that when people experience what Emerson wrote about, they will discover their greatest joy.

> "The purpose of life is not to be happy. It is to be useful, to be honorable, to be compassionate, to have it make some difference that you have lived and lived well."
>
> —*Ralph Waldo Emerson*

Recently I had dinner with advertising executive and author Linda Kaplan Thaler. You may not know her name, but I'm sure you know her work. She is the creative person who came up with the duck for AFLAC. During our dinner conversation as we talked about acts of significance, she mentioned the Hebrew phrase *tikkun olam*, and told me it means "repairing the world." She said it was part of her faith tradition and it meant that no one should live in this world without trying to find a way to make it better. What a wonderful way to think about living a life that matters.

Doing acts of significance brings more deep satisfaction than any other work I've ever known. It fires me up and keeps me going. Even when my schedule is out of control, deadlines are piling up, and the pace of life seems hectic, I seldom feel overworked. As the saying goes, work is not work unless you would rather be doing something else. There is nothing I would rather do than help people make a difference for others.

One of my favorite things I've done to help someone make a difference came to pass when a twelve-year-old boy named Kyle Beard sent me a note along with a ribbon emblazoned with the words "Who I am makes a difference." Here's what Kyle's note said:

*Dear Dr. Maxwell,*

*Hello. How are you? Is the bookmark helping? I hope so. I know you are busy planning your annual conference in Toledo, Ohio. I listened to your tapes, and I know they help others....*

*Please read the attached story.*

*My youth group is doing a project just like this story. You're supposed to take an extra ribbon and give it to somebody that makes a difference in your life to you. The reason I am giving my ribbon to you is because you have made a big difference in my life. And ever since I listened to your tape about eagles, I thought you were an eagle, too. I know you're very busy, but if you could find five minutes of your spare time to write me back and tell me who you gave your ribbon to, I would appreciate*

*it, because in order to finish the project, you have*
*to report back. I pray for you every night.*

*Your friend,*
*Kyle Beard*

*PS: I understand if you don't have time to report*
*back, but it's an honor for you to wear my ribbon.*

Kyle's message piqued my interest. So I read the
story by Helice Bridges, which was called "Who You
Are Makes a Difference." In it a high school teacher
decided to honor the seniors in her class by giving each
a ribbon imprinted with the words "Who I am makes
a difference." As she presented each, she told the student why he or she was important to her. She also gave
each student three more ribbons to hand out to others,
asking that they report back later with the results.

One of the boys pinned the ribbon on a junior
executive in appreciation for helping him with career
planning, asking him to pass along the other two ribbons. The junior executive pinned one on a surprised
boss who was known to be a bit of a grouch. The boss
took the last ribbon home and gave it to his fourteen-
year-old son.

"As I was driving home tonight I started thinking about whom I would honor with the ribbon and
I thought of you," the man said to his son. "I want
to honor you. My days are really hectic, and when

I come home, I don't pay a lot of attention to you. Sometimes I scream at you for not getting good enough grades in school, for your bedroom being a mess...but somehow, tonight, I just wanted to sit here and, well, just let you know that you do make a difference to me. Besides your mother, you're the most important person in my life. You're a great kid, and I love you."

The son broke into tears because he didn't think his father cared at all and had been considering committing suicide.[11]

After reading Helice Bridges's story, I had a deep desire to give Kyle an experience he would never forget. Instead of reporting back to him, I invited Kyle and his mom to attend one of my conferences. After challenging the audience of three thousand people to live an intentional life and make a difference, I invited Kyle to the stage. I introduced him to the crowd and then told his amazing story. I turned to Kyle and said, "Tonight I am taking your ribbon and I am challenging and passing it on to those in attendance."

I turned to the audience and asked, "How many of you would like to have a blue ribbon that says, 'Who I am makes a difference'?"

Everybody stood. My team and I happily passed out six thousand ribbons that we had created for the event—one ribbon for each attendee, plus one for each of them to pass on to someone who made a difference in their lives.

I then asked every person to hold their ribbon high as a photographer took a picture of Kyle and me with the entire audience in the background.

"Take this picture back to your youth group so they can see the results of your project," I said to Kyle.

Kyle walked off that stage to a standing ovation.

The crowd was ignited by this experience—and I was forever changed. That night it was sealed in my soul that I would intentionally make a difference for others whenever I could and show them that they could make a difference, too. That was twenty years ago, and it still makes me sing.

What do you sing about? What gives you great joy? What feeds your passion? What feeds your soul? What gets you excited?

When I ask, "What do you sing about?" many people respond by thinking about what entertains them. There's certainly nothing wrong with being entertained or having fun. I love to have fun as much as the next person. But what I'm really talking about is something that resonates at a deep level. Something that makes contented joy spontaneously rise up within you. It's the kind of thing you would do for free, just because. Once again, these are clues that help you to understand your purpose and know your *why*.

## Question 3: What Do You Dream About?

This last question really expands the possibilities of your life. It capitalizes on the answers to the two previous questions and takes them to the next level by bringing in the "what if" factor. What if you could do anything you wanted to make the world better? What if you could make a difference on a larger scale? What if you could do something significant, something that would impact others and outlast you? This is what prompted Celine Vaandrager to raise money to hire an English teacher in India. It's what made Carrie Rich think about how she could help people if she put her lunch money to work. It's what keeps me going.

In 1965 as a freshman in college, I knew I wanted to make a difference by helping people, and I wanted to do it as the pastor of a church. But to be honest, back then, I didn't dream big enough. It wasn't long before the results I was getting started to outpace my goals, and I had to reset my thinking. That may also be true for you. That's why I say that we need to start small but dream *big*.

Today, I'm dreaming bigger. I want to help a million people to achieve significance by becoming intentional in the way they live and by transforming the lives of people. And I want others to know about their stories of transformation. My greatest hope is that you will be one of those people. I want you to have a great life, full of meaning and positive impact on others. I want you to achieve a high level of significance.

I believe God gives each person a blank canvas at the beginning of his or her life. He whispers the word "purpose" as He hands us a brush and paint, and He releases us to be the artist of our own lives. He wants you to make a positive difference in the lives of many. No one else can paint your picture. The brush is in your hands; be prayerful and intentional as you choose the colors and make your strokes. As you do, He will watch with great pleasure as you paint your picture of significance.

What could your picture be? What do you dream about? If you could accomplish anything in the world that would make a difference in the lives of others, what would it be? If you could do anything you wanted and knew you wouldn't fail, what would you do? If you could live out your wildest dream, what would that look like?

Some people dream big. In fact, they're long on dreams and short on action. Others never dream. Maybe they think of themselves as pragmatic. Or maybe their hopes and dreams have been smashed by negative experiences, so they're afraid to dream. I hope that doesn't describe you. I hope you're willing and able to dream, and dream big. Even if you decide you don't want to follow through on a particular dream, the process of allowing yourself to imagine

great things is good for you. It helps you to understand who you are and why you're here.

Rabbi Harold Kushner writes, "Our souls are not
hungry for fame, comfort, wealth, or power. Those
rewards create almost as many problems as they solve.
Our souls are hungry for meaning, for the sense that
we have figured out how to live so that our lives matter, so that the world will be at least a little bit different
for our having passed through
it." What meaning does your
soul crave? How do you want
to make a difference in this
world? How can you uniquely
add value to others? What
skills do you have that can
help others' lives transform?
How can you be significant?

> "Our souls are not hungry for fame, comfort, wealth, or power.... Our souls are hungry for meaning, for the sense that we have figured out how to live so that our lives matter, so that the world will be at least a little bit different for our having passed through it."
>
> —Rabbi Harold Kushner

You may not know your
whole *why* all at once. I didn't.
But as soon as I understood
the direction I was meant to
go, I was on my way. After that, it was just a matter
of refining my *why*, which continues to happen, even
at age sixty-eight. And I hope it will continue to grow,
evolve, and sharpen. That is my signal that God's not
done with me, and there are still things for me to do
and ways for me to make a difference in this world.

## Intentional Application:
## Search Until You Find Your *Why*

### Follow the Clues

To find your *why*, you need to follow the clues that can only be found inside of you. To unlock them, take time to answer the three questions in this chapter:

*What do you cry about?*
*What do you sing about?*
*What do you dream about?*

I strongly encourage you to set aside a block of time to write out your answers to these questions. And I just want to caution you: don't try to figure out your answers before you write them down. Use the writing process to *discover* your answers. Start by writing whatever comes to mind, and just go with it. There is no right or wrong to this exercise. It's supposed to be a messy learning process. (If you're a person of faith, I also recommend you pray as you do this exercise. Ask God to reveal the clues to you.)

## Start with One Word

Another way to help you discover your *why* is to focus on the core of who you are and see what grows from that. In his book *Aspire* Kevin Hall writes, "The first thing I do when I'm coaching someone who aspires to stretch, grow and go higher in life is to have that person select the one word that best describes him or her. Once a person does that, it's as if he or she has turned to a page in a book and highlighted one word. Instead of seeing three hundred different words on the page, the person's attention, and intention, is focused immediately on that single word, that single gift. What the individual focuses on expands."[12]

What is your one word? What best describes you? That single word may inspire you, focus your attention, and help you to understand your *why*. Where will that one word take you? How does it relate to adding value to others? Why is it significant? Keep that one word in your mind as you go about your day in the coming weeks and see where it leads you.

# DOING
# SOMETHING
# THAT MAKES A
# DIFFERENCE

# 5

## Put Other People First

Margaret and I spent three years in Hillham. Those were fantastic years. We loved the people, we learned a lot, and we worked hard. When I first accepted the position, the board offered me a part-time salary because that was all they could afford to pay, but they said I was welcome to seek additional employment at the same time if I needed to. Margaret wouldn't hear of it. "John's called to lead and grow this church, and that's what he's going to do," she told the board with all the confidence of a twenty-year-old. "I'll do the extra work." She then proceeded to juggle three jobs to help us make ends meet. She taught school, worked in a jewelry store, and cleaned houses. No doubt you can tell that I married way above myself.

Word started to spread about the good things we

were doing in Hillham. People heard about our service with 301 in attendance, and they marveled that a little country church like ours had been able to grow so dramatically. Regular attendance was so good that we had to acquire land and construct a new building to hold our growing congregation.

I was also starting to receive a positive reputation for innovation and leadership. Those first stewardship materials that Margaret and I had developed were being used by other pastors with great success. I was getting to be known as an up-and-comer.

## Moving Up

I was very pleased when I received a call from the largest church in our small denomination. They were interested in hiring me to become their new pastor. It was in Lancaster, Ohio—a big step up from tiny Hillham. We saw it as a great opportunity, so we accepted the invitation and felt we were on our way.

In Hillham I had received the inspiration to build a large church. In Lancaster I felt like we were going to get the chance to actually do it. "We will build a great church here," I told the congregation after we arrived, and we set about doing exactly that.

I became increasingly aware of the need to become

a better leader during this season. I was young and full of energy. I didn't lack confidence, but I did lack experience. So I looked for help. I decided to try to connect with the pastors of the ten largest churches in America. I wanted to learn from them. But I wondered, *How do I get people like that to give time to someone like me, a kid leading a church nobody ever heard of?*

I came up with an idea. I would offer them $100 for thirty minutes of their time so that I could interview them and ask questions. That was a lot of money to us, but I was willing to invest in my ongoing growth, just as I had when I bought the kit from Curt Kampmeier. I wrote each pastor a note with my request. Two of the ten agreed to meet with me.

I went to those meetings with four or five pages of written questions. I noted the time that I arrived at their office, and as soon as I could, after the introductions and relational pleasantries, I started asking questions. I'd ask as many as I could as fast as I could and take notes. When I saw that my thirty minutes were up, I thanked them for their time and offered them the $100. I also asked them to help me to connect with those other eight large-church pastors. In the end, I got a chance to meet with all of them. For several years Margaret and I based our vacation destinations on the cities where these large churches were located, so that I could keep these appointments.

## Big Wins

Lancaster grew to be the church I had dreamed of. We helped a lot of people, and we made an impact on the community. The church grew, and once again, just as in Hillham, we were outgrowing our facilities and had to look for expansion options. We started buying up as much of the land around the church as we could. The lot closest to the church was owned by an older man named Charlie. When I first went to see him and ask about the church buying his land, he said he didn't want to sell it. "I want to die here," he told me.

I didn't pressure him. I just continued to visit him every week and build a relationship with him. After several months, one day he said, "I can tell you're helping a lot of people. Young man, I want to help you, so I am going to let you buy my land from me." So we did. And we drew up plans to build a new sanctuary and to repurpose and refurbish our existing buildings.

That same year, 1975, our church became recognized as having the fastest-growing Sunday school in the state of Ohio. That may not sound big to you, but it was huge to me. It meant my leadership had gone to another level. And people in larger pastoral circles were starting to notice, too. I was receiving recognition. It was a validation of all the hard work we were doing.

Those were heady days. My enthusiasm and emerging charisma got lots of people to join me and support my vision. And I started receiving favorable comparisons to people I admired. Because I had been born with leadership ability, I had the ability to see things before many others did, which gave me a head start in seizing opportunities and using my leadership giftedness to my advantage. I felt like I was winning all the time. And I liked it.

But there was another aspect to my personality that was threatening to limit my potential and derail me in the area of significance: my inherent competitive nature. It had been an asset when I played high school basketball, but it went to a whole new level during this season. I wanted to help people, but my motives were wrong. They were selfish. The things I was accomplishing fed my pride and my ego.

This could most easily be seen when I received the annual report of the denomination. It was a document that included the stats for every church: total attendance, the percentage the attendance grew, total annual giving, number of baptisms that had been performed, number of people serving, total Sunday school attendance—everything of note that had occurred in each church during the given year. It was a snapshot of every church in the denomination.

No matter what I was doing, no matter how busy I was, no matter how important the thing I was doing might be, the moment the annual report arrived in the mail, I stopped everything. I went off with it and spent two solid days analyzing all the numbers and comparing my church's results to everyone else's.

Where do *I* rank?

How am *I* doing?

What am *I* doing well?

What do *I* need to improve?

How do *I* stand out now?

What can *I* do to stand out more?

I was obsessed with finding out where I stood in comparison to the other churches. I became completely consumed with figuring out how I could move up and keep climbing the ladder while taking our church to the next level. I didn't stop until I had every possible scenario for personal advancement figured out.

Do you remember how I told you that when I was in Hillham, I had an inclination to hoard good ideas? Well, that desire got stronger. And I gave in to it. I leveraged every good idea to increase the size of my organization, and I didn't want to share my secrets with anybody else.

Why did I do all this? Because I wanted to win. I wanted to be first, and it felt like I could be first. I had the vision. I had the energy. I had the ability to attract people to myself and my cause. And I had the work ethic. When you have the potential to win, to be the best, how do you respond? Do you reach for it? I did!

However, there was a problem. You've probably already figured out what it was. It was all about me. All my goals and my desire to reach them were totally self-centered. I wasn't intentionally doing anything wrong, but my pursuit of success tainted my motives. I was in it for myself more than for others. I saw the stats as evidence of my success as a leader. I didn't care about the other churches. I didn't take into account that I was part of a larger team: the denomination. The only church I wanted to help was my own. And the only leader I wanted to win was me. I had been the high scorer for my high school basketball team, and I wanted to be the high scorer again.

While I don't think there's anything inherently wrong with achieving goals, charting progress, or tapping into natural competitiveness, I do think it's wrong to be self-centered, and that's what I was.

## Shifting from Success to Significance

As I look back now, I can see that significance was beginning to be within my grasp, but instead I was reaching for success. Back then I didn't get that I couldn't have a life that mattered when it was all about me and what I accomplished. I didn't really understand that significance is all about what we can do for others. Are you getting the picture?

Publisher Malcolm Forbes said, "People who matter most are aware that everyone else does, too." Think about this. Self-centeredness is the root of virtually every problem—both personally and globally. And whether we want to admit it or not, it's a problem all of us have.

> Self-centeredness is the root of virtually every problem— both personally and globally. And whether we want to admit it or not, it's a problem all of us have.

If you're tempted to believe it's not an issue for you, then let me ask a question. When you look at a group photo that you are in, who do you look for first? You look for yourself. So do I. We all look for ourselves before we look at others. If the image of us looks good, we say, "What a great picture," no matter who else might have their eyes closed, their mouths open, or their heads turned. Our opinion is based on how good we look.

So what's the problem with being a little self-centered? From my point of view, there are many. Self-centered people don't create communities that endure. Selfishly believing that we are not our brothers' keepers is not sustainable. If we want to achieve significance, then we need to become intentional about getting beyond ourselves and putting other people first. That may not stop us completely from being selfish or from thinking of ourselves first, but it will help us to curb our self-centeredness. It will help us to shift our mindset. It has been my observation that people of significance value people and can see the potential significance in each person.

I look back now and realize that as a young leader, I lived a very self-centered life. I had a "me first" attitude that showed up in many areas of my life. My competitiveness was often unbridled, and my desire to win oftentimes overwhelmed my judgment. The thing that opened my eyes to this was a conversation with Margaret in the early years of our marriage. In those days, whenever Margaret and I disagreed, I used every skill I had to win the argument. Not just occasionally, but every time. It didn't matter if the issue was large or small, philosophical or practical, personal or organizational. Every time it was a full-court press. And I won!

Have you ever been in a situation where you lost

by winning? For quite a long time, Margaret just put up with it. But then one day as I celebrated another victory, Margaret said simply, "John, you're winning the arguments, but you're losing my love."

Whoa! By winning, I was actually damaging my marriage, hurting the person I most loved. And it suddenly occurred to me if I stayed on that same path, I had the potential to lose Margaret—the love of my life and the best gift God ever gave me.

That was a wake-up call. It opened my eyes, perhaps for the first time, to how selfish and self-centered I was. I think marriage has a way of doing that to us. If you're married, maybe you agree. At any rate, that was the beginning of change for me. I wish I could say that I instantly became unselfish and never hurt Margaret's feelings again, but that wouldn't be true. However, I can say that it began a journey of change. Whenever I felt the desire to put winning ahead of my relationship with Margaret, I was *intentional* about putting her first.

That opened the door for me, and before long, I began to see my self-centeredness in other areas. So I started working on them, too. My improved attitude began to spread into these other areas of my life. As a leader, I started thinking more about others, about what they wanted and needed. It was Zig Ziglar's lesson all over again. Care about others and help them to get what they want. Do it not only because you want them to help, but because it's the way to make a difference in the world.

I honestly didn't even notice how big a difference this was making in my life until one year when the annual report arrived in the mail. Instead of dropping everything and spending two days charting my progress, I put the report to the side and thought, *I'll look at it when I have time.* It wasn't until later that I realized the significance of that act. I had grown. I still possessed high intensity. I was still curious about where I stood. But it no longer consumed me. Why? Because helping others and leading them had become more important. My focus had begun to shift. I was starting to become preoccupied with how to help others improve rather than with how to improve my personal position.

## Tapping into Significance

What drives you when you get up in the morning? Most people settle into one of three areas: survival, success, or significance. If you're like many people, you may be struggling just to keep your head above water. You're in survival mode. Whether because of circumstances, setbacks, or poor choices, you have to put a tremendous amount of effort into just making it day to day.

If you're working hard to make life better for yourself and your family, then I applaud you. Keep working. But once you've gotten to a place of stability, then what? What will you live for? Will you serve yourself or others? Will you put all of your energy into success, into trying to get farther ahead than others? Or will you work toward significance? Will you try to make a difference by helping others get ahead?

Much of my career as a speaker and writer has focused on helping people who have already achieved a level of success to find true meaning in their lives. For some that's a fairly smooth transition. For others it's not. Many people I interact with have gotten to a place where they've reached some of their financial goals—or surpassed them—which they thought would bring some kind of fulfillment. They went into their journeys thinking, "If I get more for me, I'll be happier." They thought it would bring them satisfaction and fulfillment. But they've discovered that they're still not satisfied. And in some cases, they are actually less fulfilled than when they started their journeys. Their lives feel hollow.

Many people tie their significance to their social position, their title, their net worth or bank balance, the car they drive, their prestigious address, the man or woman on their arm, or some other status symbol. Their mentality is, "If I do enough and have enough, even if I am self-centered, it will bring fulfillment." The problem is that self-centeredness and fulfillment cannot peacefully coexist. They're incompatible.

> Self-centeredness and fulfillment cannot peacefully coexist. They're incompatible.

Sometimes people struggling with this issue are uncertain about what to do. Often, they grapple with the idea of making a career change in their forties or fifties. When I encounter someone in this situation, I ask, "Do you really want to switch careers, or do you want to switch to a life that matters?" The problem usually isn't the job or career. When people are self-centered, they can make external changes, and they won't be any happier in their next career. No matter where they go, there they are.

Instead, they need to shift to significance by putting other people first. Their thinking needs to change from *What's in it for me?* to *What can I do for others?* Until that change occurs, happiness, fulfillment, and significance will always be out of their reach.

That doesn't mean success is bad. The reality is

that people must achieve a certain amount of success before they're ready for significance. They need to have found themselves, achieved something, and made themselves valuable before they have something to give to others.

> People need to have found themselves, achieved something, and made themselves valuable before they have something to give to others.

I saw this in my brother, Larry. By the time he was forty years old, he had already made enough money that he would never have to work another day in his life. He once told me his temptation was to quit working, but he knew that wouldn't make him happy. "So now I work for another reason," he told me. "I don't work for another home. I don't work for more money. All of the work I do now is going to allow me to give money away. I now work for a great cause—I work to help other people."

There's an important lesson here. Larry understood that he shouldn't leave his gift zone to get outside of himself. He shouldn't give up the thing he was best at, which was making money, so that he could do something else that didn't suit him, like becoming a missionary. He continued to use his talents for a better purpose. His money would work for him and become a river of influence to positively impact other people. That is true intentional living and true significance. He is living a life that matters.

## Making the Shift

Like Larry, to pursue a life that mattered, I had to learn to get beyond myself and think of others first. But I didn't try to get out of my strength zone. I stayed in it. I kept communicating. I kept leading a church. I kept rallying people to a greater purpose. I kept building. The main difference was that I was no longer doing it selfishly, self-centeredly. Maybe nobody else could tell the difference. But I could! My motives had changed.

For me, the process of changing was slow, and looked something like this:

> *I want to win.*
> *But too often I'm self-centered.*
> *My bent toward competitiveness and selfishness has been one of the reasons I have been successful. And my success has given me influence and privileges. I enjoy both immensely.*
> *But my success now allows me to have options. Do I go for more success? Or do I try for significance?*

*I am at a crossroad.*

*I want to use my options to add more value to me.*

*But I also want to use my options to add value to others.*

*What do I want my life to stand for? What do I want it to mean?*

*I will choose to help others.*

The first time I chose to think of others first, it was hard. But each time I made the right choice, it became a little bit easier. The selfishness was still there, but overcoming it became a little more natural. And as I became more intentional about putting others first in my life, my need to prove myself to others became less important. I began to focus on putting others first—not coming in first. I had more compelling things driving me and fulfilling me that reached far beyond me.

Are you ready to start putting other people first, not just occasionally, but as a lifestyle? It's not an easy shift to go from thinking of yourself first to thinking of others first. But it's an essential one for anyone who wants to transition from success to significance and live a life that matters. I started the shift in my twenties, but it took me until my thirties to really get it.

I hope you haven't waited as long as I did to serve others. But even if you have, you don't have to wait another day to change. It may take a while for you to work your way through your issues, just as I had to, but you can start the process today.

Or maybe you're already ahead of where I was. Maybe you're not as competitive or selfish as I was. Maybe you're more like the six-year-old daughter of a friend of mine. The mother and daughter went on a trip to Mexico serving with Homes of Hope, an organization that builds houses for needy families. While they were there, the group they were a part of took a break for lunch. To my friend's surprise, her daughter asked if she could say the prayer before the meal.

That's a remarkably confident request for a child of six in an adult environment. What's even more remarkable is that the girl had never said a prayer aloud before. But she was so moved by the experience she was having serving others that she felt compelled to ask.

"Yes," her mom said, "you can pray, but it can't be about you."

The young girl said, "Dear God. Thank you for this most excellent day. We are blessed to be together with this family here in Mexico and to be giving them a new home to live in. We hope they will be so happy in their new home. Oh, and I love my mom. Amen." This remarkable girl was already catching the vision for putting others first and serving them.

Significance is always about *others*, and serving them intentionally. When you can change your think-

> When you can change your thinking from "What am I going to receive?" to "What am I going to give?" your entire life begins to turn around.

ing from "What am I going to receive?" to "What am I going to give?" your entire life begins to turn around. And the gratification and pleasure you receive becomes deep and long lasting.

If you find it difficult to choose between doing what you want for yourself and what you should do for others, don't despair. The process takes time. Think of it like an actual wrestling match. Most winning wrestlers don't end their matches instantly. They don't pin their opponents right away. They have to work at it, and eventually, their opponent taps out or cries uncle. And then the match is over.

As you wrestle down your "want tos," you don't have to give them up quickly. Just be sure that whatever you give up, you give up for the right reasons and because you've thought it through. Otherwise you will look back with regret—or worse yet, go back and try to pick them up again. It's hard to move forward with confidence if you're looking backward.

# How to Begin Thinking of Others First

If you want help looking beyond yourself so that you start thinking of others first, I want to give you some practical advice about how to do it. But before I do, I want to be open about what made the difference for me. It was my faith, so if that offends you, just skip ahead to my first point.

As a person of faith, I am most inspired to put others first by looking at the life of Jesus. He once asked His disciples, who were bickering over position and titles, "Who would you rather be: the one who eats the dinner or the one who serves the dinner? You'd rather eat and be served, right? But I've taken my place among you as the one who serves."[13] Jesus always valued others and always put them and their needs first.

Putting others first is at the heart of my Christian faith. Having said the Lord's Prayer more times than I can count, I have realized that the prayer is very community centered. It took me years to understand that when I said the Lord's Prayer, it wasn't about me. The focus is on *us*. Yes, if we say the Lord's Prayer, we do pray for ourselves. But we also pray for others. It's a very inclusive prayer. It is a prayer that promotes a life that matters, that leads to significance. If you've prayed the prayer, think about how it starts. It says "our father," and it says "give us" not "give me."

Years ago I read this poem by Charles Royden:

*You cannot pray the Lord's Prayer, and even once
  say "I."*
*You cannot pray the Lord's Prayer, and even once
  say "my."*
*Nor can you pray the Lord's Prayer and not pray for
  another.*
*For to ask for "our" daily bread, you include your
  sister and brother!*
*All God's children are included in each and every plea.*
*From the beginning to the end of it, it does not once
  say "me."*[14]

If you're a person of faith, this may speak to you,
too. But you don't have to be a person of faith to begin
putting others first. No matter what you believe, you
probably sense that putting others first is the right
thing to do, don't you? If you want help taking steps
away from self-centeredness and toward significance,
then try doing the following:

## 1. Develop a Greater Appreciation for Other People

Recently I spoke at a conference for ATB Financial in Edmonton, Canada. Their top three hundred

leaders had gathered for a day of leadership training, and I was their keynote speaker. They had a banner draped across the stage that read, "Why We Lead—To Bring Out the Very Best in Others for Outstanding Results!" I loved that.

During the conference, Lorne Rubis, the organization's chief people officer, instructed the attendees to ask themselves this question: "Who brings out the best of me?" Right alongside the others, I took his advice. For the next thirty minutes I reflected and I wrote down the names of people who have continually added value to my life. Each time I added another name to this gratitude list, I would smile and remember something each person had said or done for me that added value to my life. Here's the list I made:

Dad showed me how to live and lead.

Mom made me feel loved every day of my life.

Margaret is my best friend who gives me great joy.

Elmer Towns sparked my dream to build a great church.

John Wooden encouraged me to make every day my masterpiece.

Andy Stanley taught me to do for one what I wish I could do for others.

Mark Cole serves me every day with a bright mind and a willing heart.

Les Parrott encouraged me to write books to extend my influence.

Coach Neff helped me to play in my sweet spot.

Paul Martinelli and Scott Fay gave me the opportunity to birth the John Maxwell Team.

Larry Maxwell helped me get started in business.

Tom Phillippe has been a trustworthy friend for over forty years.

David Hoyt took my speaking career to a higher level.

Gerald Brooks gave me the first donation to EQUIP.

Zig Ziglar encouraged me to put other people first.

Chris Hodges consistently and continually adds value to EQUIP and me.

Charlie Wetzel has been with me for twenty years helping me write books.

Robert Morris models a generous lifestyle for me.

Tom Mullins gave me the leadership lift I needed for EQUIP.

Kevin Myers developed the John Maxwell Leadership Center.

These are just a few of the people I am grateful for. My list could be endless. There isn't a week that goes by that I don't take action on something related to what was given to me by one of these people. One of my greatest motivations to add value to others is to do for others what so many have done for me.

Making such a list reminds me that I am not a self-made man. None of us can *really* claim to have done anything alone, can we? We need others. And we should value them.

Who brings out the best in you? Who are you grateful for? Have you made a list of the people you appreciate? If not, take time to compile a list like the one above. Once you have, it will be difficult for you to forget all of the people who have helped you get to where you are today, because it lives *with* you and *within* you. It lives *with* you because of the things people have done with you. It lives *within* you because of the way it sustains you. And it can inspire you to get outside of yourself and put others first, just as others have often put *you* first.

## 2. Ask to Hear Other People's Stories

In chapter one, I talked about the importance of stories and I encouraged you to recognize that your life can be a great story of significance. I hope you share in that belief, and I hope it motivates you personally. But does it motivate you to connect with others and learn their stories?

It should, because everyone you meet has a story. We can easily lose sight of this as we go about our busy days trying to get things done. So how do we counteract this? By asking people to tell us their stories. We have to slow down and take our attention off of ourselves to do that.

Do you know the stories of the people in your life? Do you know where they've come from? Are you acquainted with their struggles, their defining moments? Do you know about their hopes and dreams? Have you asked what they aspire to, and what motivates them?

It's said that Fred Rogers, of *Mr. Rogers' Neighborhood*, kept this quote in his wallet: "There isn't anyone you couldn't learn to love once you've heard their story." Don't you think that's true? I do. It's hard to remain self-centered when your focus is on others. Hearing people's stories is a great way to get outside of yourself. Not only will their stories inspire you to help them, but they will also show you *ways* you can help them.

> "There isn't anyone you couldn't learn to love once you've heard their story."
> —Fred Rogers

## 3. Put Yourself in Other People's Shoes

I read a wonderful story in the news about a couple who were in a restaurant in Iowa celebrating their anniversary. But they didn't experience the romantic evening they were hoping for. Their waiter was overwhelmed and the service was awful. It took twenty minutes to get water, forty minutes for an appetizer, and over an hour for their entrées to arrive.

People all around them were making fun of the restaurant and how bad the service was. After taking a look around, the couple noticed their server was working twelve tables by himself. The restaurant was clearly understaffed, and he was doing the best job he could under the circumstances. Despite the slow timing, the couple realized that the waiter remained upbeat, pleasant, and apologetic throughout the meal. He was absolutely delightful.

The husband and wife, who had both been servers earlier in life, recognized that the waiter had been set up to fail, and he was trying to do his best despite that. So they left him a $100 tip on a $66 tab, along with a note that simply read, "We've been in your shoes . . . paying it forward."

Because this couple had done similar work to the waiter's, they had a relatively easy time putting themselves into his shoes. But you don't need to have worked a person's job to understand where he or she is coming from. You just need to make the effort to see from that person's point of view.

How often do you intentionally put yourself in other people's shoes? Do you continually try to see the world from the point of view of others? You'll be amazed by what it can do to your perspective and your attitude.

## 4. Place Other People's Interests at the Top of Your List of Priorities

If you get to know people, appreciate them for who they are, learn their stories, and put yourself in their shoes, then you begin to understand what their interests are. What will you do with that information? Store it away hoping to use it for leverage one day? Or put it at the forefront of your thinking every day and use it to serve them?

When we get up every day, we have one of two mindsets. As you start your day, are you wondering what you will *reap*, or are you wondering what you will *sow*? Are you waiting for others to do something *for you*, or are you busy looking for something to do *for others*? People who get outside of themselves and make a difference

> **As you start your day, are you wondering what you will *reap*, or are you wondering what you will *sow*?**

are looking for ways to *sow*. They put other people's interests at the top of their list of priorities every day.

## 5. Make Winning a Group Activity

When I started my career, I thought life was an individual hundred-yard dash. But life is really more of a relay race. While winning an individual race may feel great, crossing the finish line with your team is better. Not only is it more fun, but it's also more significant.

John Wooden, who mentored me for many years, said, "Selfishness is the greatest challenge for a coach. Most players are more concerned with making themselves better than the team." The result? Seldom do the best players make the best team. Wooden described an unselfish player as one who "showed an eagerness to lose himself to the group for the goal of the team." Not only does that describe a good team member, but it also describes an intentional person who lives a life that matters by making a difference.

## Change Yourself before Expecting Change in Others

Before we leave the subject of getting outside of yourself and putting others first, I feel that I should caution you about a potential pitfall you may face as you make this shift—the desire to change people.

When I first started out in my career, I thought that helping people meant trying to change them. So I made that my goal. I wanted to teach messages that would take people to a higher place in their lives. I gave lots of advice. I was young and idealistic. I didn't yet understand that people don't change because you want them to. They change because they want to, and it happens only when they're ready to.

If we want to help others, then we must first help ourselves. If we want to change the world, then we must change. People can't be agents of change unless they've gone through positive change themselves. I learned that I had to travel within before I traveled without. In other words, I had to make some changes in myself before I could expect to effect change in others. I could not give what I did not have. If I wanted to see others transformed, I had to be transformed. I had to do the hard work myself.

This ultimately contributed to my shift from teacher to leader. I realized that if I changed, then put others' needs above my own and cared more about their wants than my own, I could make an impact. I could speak as a friend, as one who had been in the trenches, who had been where they are.

It is also one of the reasons that when I speak today

I use so many personal illustrations. I know it's the most effective way to connect with people. All of my conviction and confidence comes from talking about things that happened to me. When I speak about my experiences, people relate mine to how their own experiences have affected them.

The power of personal transformation to help others can be seen in Global Teen Challenge, an organization that helps kids get off drugs. I serve on an advisory board to them, and when I hear the stories of transformation, it amazes and inspires me. Their organization's success rate is close to 70 percent, while that of others trying to do the same things is closer to 18 percent.

Curious about the staggering difference, I asked the president of Global Teen Challenge about it at one of our meetings. He responded, "Almost all the people that do the teaching for Global Teen Challenge are former drug addicts. We don't bring in people who have studied the drug issue. We don't bring in educators to talk to people. There's tremendous change that happens in someone's life when the person who's trying to help them out of the ditch had to get out of the ditch him- or herself."

There is an amazing amount of motivation, hope, and credibility when someone has been there, done that, and gone on to become successful. If the person telling you to get off drugs hasn't been through the experience, there's no common ground—or credibility. If they have done drugs, yet kicked the habit, they stand on higher ground saying, "Come up to where I am standing."

Recently I came across a story about a man who went through a dramatic change when he took the time to get outside of himself and think about others in a way he hadn't before. Described as one of the world's most powerful and influential financiers and reportedly making $100 million a year, he quit his job.[15] Why would he do that? Because of a note he received from his daughter.

The man is Mohamed El-Erian, and he was the CEO of PIMCO, an investment firm that manages more than $2 trillion in investments. One day El-Erian asked his young daughter to do a chore, and she didn't get started with it right away. When he began to hold her accountable for it, she went to her room and brought him a list she had already made of all the events that were important to her that her dad had missed. It included her first day of school, her first soccer match of the season, a parent-teacher meeting, and a Halloween parade—twenty-two items in all. "And the school year wasn't yet over," says El-Erian.

For perhaps the first time in his life, he was seeing things from his daughter's point of view. It left an indelible impression upon him. He got up every morning before dawn and worked late. And he traveled extensively. He spent very little time with his daughter. So he made a critical decision. He would put his daughter first. In January of 2014, he told PIMCO he would leave the company in March.

After El-Erian made the transition, he described it like this:

Earlier this year I left behind the privilege and intellectual stimulation of working with extremely talented colleagues and friends at PIMCO and instead opted for a portfolio of part-time jobs that requires a lot less travel and offers a ton more flexibility—enough, I hope, to allow me to experience with my daughter more of those big and little moments that make up each day.[16]

Now El-Erian alternates days with his wife, getting up with his daughter, cooking her breakfast, and taking her to school. I think he understands that if he doesn't seize this opportunity to make a difference in his daughter's life, he won't get it back later.

It can be very difficult for many of us to get beyond ourselves and begin putting others first. I know it's been difficult for me. Do you find it difficult too? I believe the stronger a person's drive and the bigger his or her personality, the more difficult it can be. But if someone like El-Erian—a PhD educated at Cambridge and Oxford with one of the most high-profile jobs in the world—can do it, then there's hope for all of us.

El-Erian acknowledges that not everyone can afford to quit his or her job to spend more time at home. But that's not the key change. What needs to change are our hearts. What must transform are our attitudes. What must be purified are our motives. We can't allow our lives to be all about us. That's not the way to do something that makes a difference. If we want to choose significance, we must put other people first.

# Intentional Application: Put Other People First

## Who Makes Your List?

Take some time to think about who has helped you in your life, and then make a gratitude list. Be sure to include at least ten people, but don't limit yourself to only ten if you can think of more. (If you can't think of ten, that is a clue about your attitude toward others and a possible inability to get outside of yourself.) For each person whose name you put on the list, write how that person has helped you and why it has been important to you.

## Look for Clues in People's Stories

Do you know the stories of the people in your life? Not just the stories of close family members, but also of your employees, co-workers, clients, neighbors, and friends? If not, make it your goal to ask at least one person to tell you his or her story this week and every week until you've heard them all. Listen not only to learn their histories, but also to discover their hopes, dreams, and aspirations. Make notes if needed to help you remember. And try to identify specific ways you would be able make their interests one of your priorities.

## Harness Your Success for Significance

In this chapter I discussed how my brother Larry didn't walk away from doing the things that made him successful in order to achieve significance. Instead, he shifted his focus to using his gifts and talents to benefit others.

Make a list of your top successes, your big wins based on your best skills, talents, and opportunities. You may come up with only one or two things, or your list may be quite extensive. Then think about how you could harness that success to help others. Could you use it as a springboard to help people? Could you teach others how to succeed using your experience? Has it given you resources or opportunities that you could share with someone else? Be creative. Significance comes from using what you have to benefit others.

# 6

## Add Value to Others from Your Sweet Spot

It was the worst day of my young life as a pastor. Benny Harris, a board member and leader of the Hillham congregation, called me in Lancaster to share with me that my former church in Hillham was not doing well. Six months after I had left, the attendance had fallen from three hundred to less than a hundred. Benny's voice was broken as he asked, "What's gone wrong?"

I had no answers for him. And I felt empty for not knowing how to respond.

I went outside and walked around trying to clear my head. I felt terrible. I kept asking myself the same question, "What went wrong?"

When I made the transition from the small church

in Hillham to the larger church in Lancaster, I felt very satisfied and proud of my accomplishments at that first church. My reputation in the small Hillham church was like that of Superman, leaping tall buildings and growing the congregation from the ground up—from three to over three hundred.

I had worked so hard to grow the congregation. I had cared for those people as well as I could. A beautiful new church building had been built on a knoll, and it was filling up week after week before I left. Why was it slowly emptying after my departure? My sense of prideful self-satisfaction came crashing down quickly.

*What happened?* I wondered.
*How could it all fall apart so fast?*
*Why did it fall apart?*
*Who was to blame?*

In my early twenties, I was long on energy, but short on practical experience. It took me six months of thinking through all the possibilities of what went wrong, until it hit me like a ton of bricks. I finally figured out the problem. And when I did, I became even more discouraged by the realization.

The problem was me!

Have you ever racked your brain to solve a problem only to discover that you were the cause? There is nothing worse than that. But that was where I found myself.

What happened was actually a common rookie leadership mistake. I had done all the work myself in that little church. Well, not just me. Margaret and I did the work. She handled the youth, missions, special projects, and hospitality. I led the church, preached, visited people, recruited new people, developed programs, and handled problems.

As the congregation grew, I felt like a local rock star. My Volkswagen Beetle ran nonstop on those dusty dirt roads doing "God's business" for the community. People were enthralled by my boundless energy, wondering, "How does he get it all done?" As my reputation got bigger, unfortunately, so did my head. When pastors asked me how I was developing that little country church, I would proudly say, "I work hard." Then I would go into great detail about the importance of working longer hours, putting in sweat equity, and paying the price if they wanted to build a great church.

I didn't have a clue. I'm embarrassed by that now.

Never once did I invest in people. I had loved the people, but I had never added value to them. After I left Hillham, many people were really no better off than they had been before I arrived there.

I hadn't trained anyone to take over in my absence. While I was busy building my career, I didn't include other people along the way. Everyone around me was happy to let me do it all. More than that, they *loved* me for it. And I gladly accepted the applause because I thought that was what a good leader was supposed to do—work harder than everyone else and accept the accolades.

Boy, was I wrong. I had built everything around *myself,* so when I left, it all fell apart. It was a fast fall, too. I didn't realize what I had done until after I got the news from Benny. It was a result of my inexperience and naïveté.

After licking my ego wounds for a few weeks, I had to figure out how to begin to fix what was broken in me. I didn't want to continue making the same mistakes as I went forward. Anything of real significance is lasting. It doesn't fall apart quickly once it no longer has your attention. That's especially true if you're a leader. The true measure of success is succession—what happens after you're gone.

I started to think about what I needed to do. The first step in my recovery was clear. I had to admit to myself that I was not indispensable. And I had to stop doing things that made me *feel* indispensable. I needed to shift my focus. Instead of making a difference *for* people, I would work to make a difference *with* people. Instead of doing things to emphasize my value, I would focus on making others more valuable.

The pathway seemed clear to me. I would start by equipping people so that no matter what happened to me, they could carry on and make a difference. I would ask others to join me in doing the work and in leading, and I would add value to them. That would not only show them that I cared for them, it would help to develop them as individuals, improve their quality of life, and give them new skills that would benefit them, the organization, and others.

Although the shift from making a difference *for* people to making a difference *with* people may sound like a subtle switch in behavior, it was actually a radical shift in my approach. When I arrogantly thought I was the entire picture, I could never see the bigger picture. As John Holmes said, "It is well to remember that the entire universe, with one trifling exception, is composed of others." But once I realized that my focus needed to be on others and on adding value to them, I was able to multiply my impact, fine-tune my purpose, and work within my best gifts.

## Becoming Intentional in Adding Value

If you want to be significant and live a life that matters, you must add value to others. I know I'm repeating myself, but I have to say it again: significance and selfishness don't go together. You cannot be a selfish,

> **If you want to be significant and live a life that matters, you must add value to others.**

self-centered person and live a life that matters. You have to take the focus off of yourself and put it on making the lives of others better.

*What* you must do to be significant is consistent for everyone. You must add value. *How* you do that is as unique as you are. It begins with knowing your *why*. But it continues with your unique gifts and talents, opportunities and resources. My two greatest gifts are communication and leadership. Where those two intersect is where I add the most value. It's my sweet spot. Why do I communicate? To add value to people. Why do I lead? To add value to people. That's how I make a difference.

When someone comes to me and says he wants to become a leader or communicator, one of the first questions I ask is, why? Why do you want to become a leader? Is it because you want a corner office? Is it for a premium parking place or a top salary? Is it for the perks and recognition? Why do you want to become a communicator? Is it so that you can be onstage and have fans? All of these are wrong motives. If anyone wants to become a leader or communicator for any reason other than adding value, he's off base.

For most people who don't add value to others,

their actions aren't motivated by hate or even self-centeredness—they're usually caused by *indifference*. However, no one can be indifferent and live a life of significance. We have to *want* to make life better for others.

Many people do that too casually. They are prompted by circumstances. They see a person in trouble and stop to help. Or a friend calls needing assistance and they respond. That's good. But there is another, higher level of adding value that significant people embrace. It's intentional. It's proactive. It's a lifestyle.

People of intentional significance make it their everyday goal to add value to people using their best gifts, skills, and resources. It's part of their *purpose*. They are always actively looking for ways to make the lives of other people better.

Many of my friends do this. Real estate broker Dianna Kokoszka sets alerts on her phone twice a day. In the morning, an alert pops up with this question: "Who will you add value to today?" At 8:00 p.m. the alert asks, "How did you add value to others today?" If she feels that she hasn't added value to someone that day, she doesn't go to bed until she has.

Entrepreneur and author Chris Estes sends a one-minute phone message of encouragement to five people every day. Businessman and EQUIP board member Colin Sewell writes three personal notes every day. You don't have to be a superstar or an over-achiever to add value to people. You just need to care and begin doing something about it.

English novelist George Eliot said, "Try to care about something in this vast world besides the grati-fication of small selfish desires. Try to care for what is best in thought and action—something that is good apart from the accidents of your own lot. Look on other lives besides your own. See what their troubles are, and how they are borne." No doubt Eliot was striving to live a life of significance.

## The Five Essential Values of Adding Value to Others

Do you have the desire to help other people and add value to them? If so, is it intentional and stra-tegic? Are you willing to cultivate the desire so that it is more proactive? If so, there are five important insights about adding value to others that will help you. They helped strengthen my commitment to and vision of serving others, and I believe they will do the same for you.

## 1. To Add Value to Others I Must First Value Myself

As parents, Margaret and I realized when our children were young that we couldn't teach them everything, so we came up with five essential principles we wanted to pass along that would help them be successful and feel good about who they are. We wanted to ground them in faith, responsibility, unconditional love (so they would know what it's like to prosper and thrive), gratitude, and self-worth.

We included self-worth because we understood that it's impossible to consistently behave in a way that is inconsistent with how we feel about ourselves on the inside. Self-image dictates daily behavior. How we see ourselves regulates what we consistently do, and our regular behavior is what defines us, not what we might do on a rare occasion.

The ability to add value to others has to be based on more than just saying, "I value people." It must be built upon the solid ground of believing in ourselves. The only way we can be consistent and authentic in valuing others is to see value in ourselves.

I explain this in my book *Winning with People* using the Lens Principle. It says that who we are determines how we see others. In other words, we don't see people as *they* are; we see people as *we* are. Speaker and author Brian Tracy said it this way: "There is a direct relationship between your own level of self-esteem and the health of your personality. The more you like and respect yourself, the more you like and respect other people. The more you consider yourself to be a valuable and worthwhile person, the more you consider others to be valuable and worthwhile as well. The more you accept yourself just as you are, the more you accept others just as they are."

Observers of human behavior have learned that people with low self-esteem are almost always self-centered and preoccupied with their own thoughts and actions. In contrast, people who help others tend to feel good about the people they help and to feel good about themselves. When you add value to others, there is an instant return of positive emotions that causes you to feel better about who you are. Haven't you experienced those positive feelings when you've helped someone in need?

Positive thinking doesn't build self-image. Positive acts do. There's nothing wrong with positive thinking, but the most effective way to cross over into intentional living is to think positive thoughts that ultimately turn into positive acts. If you perform positive acts, not only will your self-image begin to rise, you will find yourself living a more significant life that matters.

When our children were young, Margaret and I had an annual Christmas project. We would find a cause and give ourselves to it. Or we would look for a family in need and provide a nice Christmas for them. When we were finished, our children always wanted to know when they could do this kind of thing again, and they started asking what we were going to do the next year. Invariably, these efforts were always the highlight of our Christmas season. Why? Because we were intentional in adding value to others, and the positive action not only built their self-esteem but also added value to us.

If you only place a small value upon yourself, rest assured that the rest of the world will not raise the price. And as a result of your own low self-esteem and poor sense of self-worth, you will fail to make a positive difference in the lives of others because you'll think you have little to offer.

If you're wondering whether you value yourself enough to add value to others, then think about this. You know you truly value yourself when each day you silently affirm that you are the type of person with whom you would like to spend the rest of your life. If you don't feel that way,

> You know you truly value yourself when each day you silently affirm that you are the type of person with whom you would like to spend the rest of your life.

then you still have some work to do in the inside to be in the best position to help others.

## 2. To Add Value to Others I Must Value Others

Mother Teresa said, "One of the greatest diseases is to be nobody to anybody." As a pastor, I spent a lot of time visiting people in nursing homes over the years. One of the heartbreaks for me was the people I saw who never had family visiting them. *Does anybody even know they're here?* I'd wonder. *Does anyone even care?*

When I did weekly hospital visits, I would often check in with the front desk to see if there were any people who had not been visited by anyone since my last call. And I did my best to look in on those who'd had no visitors. I didn't always get to everyone, but I surely tried.

Recently while I was speaking in San Diego, a friend gave me a copy of a poem that has made the rounds on the Internet. It was originally written in 1966 by a nurse named Phyllis McCormack, who worked with geriatric patients. When I read the words, it spoke to me because of my experiences in hospitals and nursing homes:

*What do you see nurse, what do you see?*
*What are you thinking when you look at me,*
*A crabby old woman, not very wise,*
*Uncertain of habit with far away eyes,*
*Who dribbles her food, and makes no reply,*
*When you say in a loud voice: "I do wish you'd try."*
*Who seems not to notice the things that you do,*
*And forever is losing a stocking or shoe,*
*Who, quite unresisting, lets you do as you will*
*With bathing and feeding, the long day to fill.*
*Is that what you're thinking, is that what you see?*
*Then open your eyes, you're not looking at me.*
*I'll tell you who I am, as I sit here so still,*
*As I move at your bidding, as I eat at your will,*
*I'm a small child of ten, with a father and mother,*
*And brothers and sisters, who love one another,*
*A girl of sixteen, with wings on her feet,*
*Dreaming that soon a lover she'll meet;*
*A bride soon at twenty my heart gives a leap,*
*Remembering the vows that I promised to keep;*
*At twenty-five now I have young of my own,*
*Who need me to build a secure, happy home;*
*A woman of thirty, my young now grow fast,*
*Bound together with ties that should last;*
*At forty, my young sons have grown up and gone;*
*But my man stays beside me to see I don't mourn;*

*At fifty once more babies play 'round my knee;*
*Again we know children, my loved one and me.*
*Dark days are upon me, my husband is dead,*
*I look at the future, I shudder with dread.*
*For my young are all busy, with young of their own,*
*And I think of the years and the love I have known.*
*I'm an old woman now, and nature is cruel,*
*'Tis her jest to make old age look like a fool.*
*The body, it crumbles, grace and vigor depart,*
*There is a stone where I once had a heart.*
*But inside this old carcass, a young girl still dwells,*
*And now and again my battered heart swells.*
*I remember the joys, I remember the pain,*
*And I'm loving and living all over again.*
*I think of the years, all too few and gone too fast,*
*And accept the stark fact that nothing can last.*
*So open your eyes, nurse, open and see,*
*But a crabby old woman, look closer, see me.*[17]

How often do we look past others, not really seeing who they are? Not getting to know them? Not
valuing them as individuals? Every person has value,
and to be people who live lives that matter, we need
to intentionally value others and express that value to
them. It's not optional if we desire to be significant.

### 3. To Add Value to Others I Must Value What Others Have Done for Me

One Thanksgiving a few years ago when our grandchildren were very young, Margaret and I decided to help them put on a Thanksgiving Day play for the whole family. Margaret was in charge of the costumes, I was the producer and director (I bet that's a surprise!), and the children were the talent. As I led them through rehearsal, they practiced their songs and memorized various inspirational quotes about Thanksgiving. Our grandson, little John, was five years old at the time. His only line was, "We all should have an attitude of gratitude."

The morning of the play he came to me to practice his line. He kept saying "gratitude" before "attitude." After a few times trying to get it right, he was flustered and tired. Falling down on the floor he looked up at me and said, "This gratitude stuff is exhausting."

I laughed at his hilarious delivery, and then I immediately rewrote his part to include his statement with the dramatics of falling down. Later I thought, "Gratitude isn't supposed to be exhausting. It's supposed to be invigorating!" But of course, when we put gratitude before attitude, it can be exhausting.

If you don't have an attitude of gratitude on Thanksgiving Day, then it is going to be hard to be appreciative any day of the year. Gratitude is the motivation for doing good things for others, and a positive attitude is what drives that action. Gratitude fuels us to want to do good things for others.

Have you ever met people who think nothing good ever happens to them? It's like they walk around with dark clouds over their heads, and they always say things like, "No one ever gives me a chance. I never get a break. Why doesn't anyone ever pick me?" Such people live very self-consuming, selfish lives. How can they experience significance at all?

We've all heard the expression, "Count your blessings." But have you ever stopped to wonder what that really means? When we count our blessings and realize what others have done for us, it stimulates us to say, "I want to do something for someone else." You have to count your blessings before you can be a blessing.

### 4. To Add Value to Others I Must Know and Relate to What Others Value

In this world, I believe we all have *one* thing we are really best at. For me, that's communication. I believe my strength in communication is being other-person focused, not being focused on myself. It's why I always do my best to connect with my audience.

When most speakers finish, they want to know how they did. They wonder, *Did the audience like me? How did I do?* That's not how I think. When I'm done speaking, I am only interested in knowing one thing. Did I help the people? The best and most effective way I can serve others through my speaking is if the message helped them.

Early in my career, I came to the conclusion that all great speakers lose themselves in their audience. They have one desire, and that is to connect with people. You can't connect with an audience if you're above them. If you look down on people, you won't want to raise them up. But that psychological truth also comes into play physically. I like being down where the people are, so whenever possible, I get off the platform. I leave the stage and walk among the crowd. It takes away barriers. If you move toward people, they move toward you. If you move away from people, they pull back, too.

If you want to impress people, talk about your successes. But if you want to impact people, talk about your failures. Telling self-deprecating stories in a conversational style helps me get to a place where I can communicate with people in a way that makes them feel comfortable, without my coming off as authoritarian. And that's when I have the best chance of adding value to them. Everything I do when I speak is intentional. But I'm sure that does not come as a surprise. By now you know intentionality is a lifestyle I've practiced for many years.

In 2010 I wrote a book called *Everyone Communicates, Few Connect.* In it I describe connecting practices that we can use to better connect with others. The first connecting principle is to find common ground. When we first meet someone, there is a relationship gap between us. We don't know them, they don't know us. Who will be the first to close that gap? The one who finds common ground. How do you do that? By embracing these seven qualities and practices:

- Availability—I will choose to spend time with others.
- Listening—I will listen my way to common ground.
- Questions—I will be interested enough in others to ask questions.
- Thoughtfulness—I will think of others and how to connect with them.
- Openness—I will let people into my life.
- Likeability—I will care about people.
- Humility—I will think of myself less so I can think of others more.

Years ago I made a conscious decision to be the person who intentionally initiates connection with others and finds common ground. But sometimes I have to really fight for it. Some people see me as a celebrity, and they think I'm different from them. I call that the success gap. It can happen whenever a person is seen as successful or famous. Others believe there is a gap between that individual and themselves.

I first recognized that people were seeing me differently when they started asking for my autograph or to take a picture with me. At first I was exhilarated to have admirers. But soon I started to see the gap, which I realized could prevent me from adding value to people. So I do what I can to stay connected to people and help them realize I'm just a flawed person doing his best, just like everyone else.

In 2013 when I was speaking in Guatemala on the subject of values, the security team and other VIPs sometimes tried to keep me away from people before and after I spoke. But I wanted to be among the people who came to see me speak. I wanted to shake hands, answer questions, and take pictures with everyone who wanted to meet me. Unless someone told me I was in danger, I also planned to sit in the crowd when others were presenting. I didn't want anyone there to get the impression that I thought I was better than they were—because I am not. Not only did I need to connect with the Guatemalan people to make my trip successful, I also *wanted* to connect with them. Doing this helped add value to them, and it showed how deeply I cared about what they valued. It also added value to me because I met many wonderful people. I have never been the kind of speaker who is interested in *fans*. I want *friends*.

Do you know and relate to what others value? Do you go out of your way to connect with others? It doesn't have to be anything big. You can connect with people in simple ways. Get to know your neighbors and do something nice for them. Learn the name of your waitress and leave her a good tip. Talk with children to find out what's important to them, and then praise and encourage them. Do what you can wherever you are.

## 5. To Add Value to Others I Must Make Myself More Valuable

The idea of adding value to people is dependent on the fact that you have something of value to give them. Adding value to someone is relatively easy to do once. But what if you want to add value to others every day of your life for as long as you live? To do that, you must continually grow and become more valuable. And to add the most value, you should try to stay in your sweet spot.

Each of us right now has a lid on our potential. The only way to lift that lid is to intentionally develop and grow. As you do this you will make a wonderful discovery—you can also lift the lids of others. I have always considered myself to be a lid lifter—someone who sees the greatest potential in others and then gives them what they need to rise up and fly.

I found this to be true in Lancaster. As I equipped and trained people to do specific tasks, I started to get additional opportunities to add value to them in other ways. I helped them to become better leaders. I challenged them to strive for excellence in other areas of their lives. I helped them improve the important relationships in their lives. And I supported them as they fought to strengthen their characters. Every time I learned a new skill or fought a personal battle, I had more to give. As I improved myself, I helped others to improve, too.

As I was writing these words, I just stopped long enough to send a text to a company where we are training seven hundred of their leaders. We are helping them "lift their lid" so they can do the same for others. Here is what I wrote:

For forty years I have led people through the growth program you will begin tonight. Here are the lessons I've learned over those years.

1. **No shortcuts.** You only cheat yourself and everyone you are leading.
2. **In every exercise use A-C-T.** Note and do the things you should *Apply, Change, and Teach* others. Practicing what you are learning is the only way you will grow while you are learning.
3. **Think long-term.** This is not a "quick fix" endeavor. Leaders develop daily, not in a day.
4. **Think beyond yourself.** Your goal is to get better so you can help your team get better. If you want to add, do it yourself. If you want to multiply, take others with you.
5. **Have fun.** I define growth as happiness. My team promises to give you what you need to help you become what you want to be! We are 100 percent with you. No excuses. Together we can make a difference! This is your chance to do something that will be a strong inspiration to thousands. Get in the story! You are the story!

Although I sent those words to others, they also apply to you. Grow yourself—grow others. Learn for yourself—then pass it on. Lift your lid so that you can lift others'!

## Knowing How You Can Add Value

Do you agree that adding value to people has high value? Can you see that being intentional about it is a key to living a life of significance and having a life that matters? If so, then you're probably wondering *how* you should try to add value. To know the answer, ask yourself these three questions:

### What Have I Been Given? (Looking Backward)

I've benefitted from many things in my life. One of them was seeing the excellent model of significance in my parents. Every day I saw them helping others. I was also given extraordinary encouragement to help people by others along the way. As a result, I wanted to come alongside others and help them go to higher levels in their lives. Each time I was able to do this, I was putting wins of significance under my belt. Each victory built my confidence and conviction—confidence that I would live a significant life and conviction that others could, too. The more I built both, the more inspired I was to keep doing the work and living a life of intentionality.

What experiences have you had that have uniquely equipped you to add value to others? Those experiences could be positive, as mine were, or they could be difficulties or negative circumstances that you have overcome. I know people who have had eating disorders and were able to come alongside others who struggled with that same issue and help them. I've known people who have made fortunes who used their money to build villages, rescue orphans, and construct hospitals. I know people with a knack for business who have helped budding entrepreneurs in developing countries.

What accomplishments, resources, and experiences can you draw upon? What wisdom have you gained through the crucible of personal loss or tragedy? What can you draw upon to help others and add value to them?

## What Do I Have to Give? (Looking Inward)

Everyone has qualities, talents, and skills that have the potential to add value to others. One of the things I possess is boundless energy. My life is filled with great passion—even in my late sixties—and I love to encourage people. Encouragement is something I give everyone I can every day of my life. I learned it from my father. I once asked him to help me know and understand whom I should encourage.

"Son," he told me with a smile, "if they are breathing, they need to be encouraged."

So I had it modeled for me, but it's also deep within me. I naturally put a "ten" on people's heads, meaning I see them at their best. I believe everyone can become someone. Everyone can live with significance.

I also have the ability to communicate. I've talked a lot about this. And I can lead. These are things I do naturally every day. They aren't work for me. Don't get me wrong, I still work at them. But it's a pleasure.

What is inside you that can help you make others better? What skills do you possess? What talents have been given to you? What personality traits do you have that can be used to add value to others? *Anything* and *everything* you have can be used to help others if you make adding value to people your priority and become intentional about it.

## What Can I Do? (Looking Outward)

Every day I can be intentional in adding value to people's lives. Every day I can look at my schedule and ask myself, "Who can I help today? How can I help them? When should I do that?" You can do that same thing.

Looking outward with an eagerness to add value to others influences how you will see people. We usually see only what we are prepared to see in others and the world. That's why two people can be in the same place, in the same circumstances, surrounded by the same people, and see the same thing completely differently.

You don't have to go halfway around the world to add value to people. You don't need to start a nonprofit organization. You don't have to get an advanced degree. You just need to keep your eyes open and be intentional about it.

In Lancaster, I started where I was with the people I had, teaching them what I knew. I immediately started training them to do things they wanted to do. That became my main focus. And I developed a process that I still use to this day:

**Model—I do it.** Before I try to teach someone else, I work to become good at it so that I know what I'm doing.

**Mentor—I do it and you watch.** Learning begins when I show someone how to do what I do. I learned in Lancaster never to work alone. No matter what task I was doing, I always tried to take with me someone who wanted to learn.

**Monitor—You do it and I watch.** Nobody learns how to do something well on the first try. People need to be coached. When others do the task and I'm there to watch, I can help them troubleshoot problems and improve.

**Motivate—You do it.** I always try to hand off tasks as soon as possible and encourage the people I've trained. I become their biggest cheerleader.

**Multiply—You do it and someone else is with you.** This is the final step. I don't want the equipping cycle to end with me. I want it to continue. When I train someone to do something, I want them to turn around and train someone else, just as I did them.

Who is already in your life that you can add value to? What can you do to help them? Opportunities are all around you. That's one of the reasons significance is within your reach today, right now. All you have to do is be willing to act. What do you have to give? What can you help someone else to learn? How can you make life better for others? What you have to give is unique. What's your sweet spot? No one else can give what you can give.

## Finding What He Was Meant to Do

There is a professional photographer from Britain named Giles Duley whose story I just became acquainted with. Duley started his career as a photographer taking pictures of musicians. He soon added fashion models and celebrities to his portfolio. For ten years he traveled throughout Europe and America taking photos, his work regularly appearing in *GQ*, *Esquire*, and *Vogue*. However, even though he was highly successful, he felt like he was wasting his life. He wanted to do something more, something significant. He wanted to make a difference.

So what did Duley do? He gave up photography and took a position as a full-time caregiver—someone whose job is to take care of a person with disabilities around the clock. His client was a young man with severe autism named Nick, whom he looked after for several years.

It was a challenge for Duley. Nick described his life as being like living downstairs from a party where he could hear people and perceive that they were having a good time in the kitchen, but he was trapped in the basement and could never go upstairs and join the party.

Duley started taking photos of Nick to document his life. He didn't really plan to do anything with the photos. But there was an issue with Nick that changed that. Nick used to injure himself. When he got frustrated, he would punch himself in the face until he was bruised, gashed, and bloody. When Duley tried to get Nick some help, his concerns were dismissed. It wasn't until Duley took a photo of Nick's battered face that social services was finally willing to help him.

That's when Duley realized he had the ability to tell someone's story with his photography. And it inspired him to go out and do exactly that. He started traveling with his camera again. He went to Kutupalong in Bangladesh near the border of Myanmar, where thousands of people were living in and around refugee camps. He lived for a short time with street kids in Odessa, Ukraine. He went to South Sudan and Angola.

He is captivated by people's stories, and he wants to capture and retell those stories by using photographs. He says he wants to tell the untold stories of forgotten people whose lives matter. A reporter for the *Observer* says that Duley aims at what's universal, and his real gift is empathy.[18]

Duley's travels also took him to Afghanistan, because he wanted to tell the story of what war does to soldiers. He spent weeks with an American army unit, and he felt he wasn't getting the story he hoped to tell. Then one day when he was out on patrol with the soldiers, he stepped on an IED, which blew off one arm and both legs. The soldiers, who were combat veterans, heroically managed to save his life. Though he survived, it devastated him and he thought his work was over. But as his recovery progressed, he had a realization.

"I went to those places," Duley said, "because I wanted to make some kind of change, and photography was my tool. Then I became aware that my body was a living example of what war does to somebody. In other words, I could use my own experience, my body to tell that story."[19]

He not only did that, but he also went back out to take pictures, including in Afghanistan. This time he wanted to capture the story of how war affected civilians, including those who lost limbs. Duley even rigged a contraption that he could hook onto what remained of his left arm to hold his camera. "My friends love this idea of me as half man, half camera," Duley jokes.[20]

Duley's resilience, strength, and humor are admirable, I'm sure you'll agree. But it's vital not to miss the most important detail of his story. He is making a difference from his sweet spot—photography—not in some other way. He didn't move away from his strength to make a difference. He moved back toward it.

Duley explains, "I was lucky ten years ago when I sat down and I tried to work out what I could do to make a difference in this world. I realized that my photography was a tool and a way to do it. I think that what's really key is that we can all be...cogs in a wheel of change. We can all make a difference. Everybody has an ability to use something to make a difference in the world."

We can all add value to people. And the biggest difference we can make will come from our sweet spot. We should not leave what we do best. We should stay with our best to give our best—and make the greatest impact.

There is a passage in the book *Souls on Fire* by Elie Wiesel in which he writes that when you die and you meet your Maker, you're not going to be asked why you didn't become a Messiah or find a cure for cancer. All you're going to be asked is, "Why didn't you become you? Why didn't you become all that you are?" To become all you are, you must use your best to add value to people.

Leo Buscaglia wrote, "Choose the way of life. Choose the way of love. Choose the way of caring. Choose the way of hope. Choose the way of belief in tomorrow. Choose the way of trusting. Choose the way of goodness. It's up to you."

## Finding My Sweet Spot

One of the great ironies of life is that if you give up your life, you gain it. If you help others, you benefit. If you lose yourself, you find yourself.

When I started leading for the benefit of others and adding value to them instead of being selfish, a whole other world opened up to me. And I can tell you the exact place and exact moment it happened.

It was while I was speaking at an outdoor rally on July 4, 1976. I was leading a bicentennial celebration for a group of about three thousand people. While I was speaking, I experienced an overwhelming sense, an inner calling to not just lead others, but to train leaders. It was like God whispered it in my ear. I know that may sound a little mystical, but it was as clear as anything I've experienced in my entire life.

On the way home I described the experience to Margaret, and she asked, "What are you going to do about it?"

My inner confidence that it would happen was so strong that I responded, "Nothing. I'm going to wait to see how it plays out."

Within weeks of the event, I started receiving calls from leaders asking me to train them in leadership.

I had come to love leadership and leading, but *training* new leaders was out of my wheelhouse. After all, I was a pastor. My education was in theology. It would mean a whole new world for me. I would have to grow to a new level, acquire new skills, and plan my life differently. I knew I would have to reinvent myself. So I got started.

I spent a lot of time thinking about what leaders needed and where they struggled. I started thinking in terms of leadership principles and practices that I could teach to others. I began creating leadership systems. I studied different kinds of communicators and how they approached training people in various settings. And I began developing a new style of communication that was different from preaching.

I can tell you now that reinventing myself is something I have had to do several times in my life as I felt called to greater tasks. It's always a challenge, but an enjoyable one. I love learning and developing new skills. But no matter what new mountain I face, I always stay close to the one thing I do best—communicate. That's my key to being able to continue adding value to people. I stay in my strength zone as I leave my comfort zone. This is one of the ways you fine-tune your sweet spot.

In his book *Geeks & Geezers*, Warren Bennis writes, "Every leader, regardless of age, went through at least one intense transformational experience." And this was definitely my first big one. Forty years later,

I can look back and say that bicentennial celebration was a truly pivotal day in my life.

Why?

Every time I train leaders, I think, *This is what I was made for.*

## Identifying Your Sweet Spot

What were you made for?

All my talk about leadership and communication may make you think I'm telling you that you must become a leader or public speaker. I hope you haven't gotten that impression. I don't tell you my story to try to make you think you should be more like me. To the contrary, you need to become more like *you*!

> You need to become more like *you*!

Where is your sweet spot for helping others and adding value to them? What's the thing you can do that will make a difference in the world? What are you passionate about? What can you do that resonates so deeply in your soul that when you do it, you *know* your life is significant?

If you don't already know what it is, then follow the steps I've already outlined in this book to begin discovering it:

- **Get into your story.** Decide that you *can* make a difference, and become the hero of your own life.
- **Become highly intentional.** Be determined to make every day count by being proactive in making a difference.
- **Start small but believe big.** Take action as Carrie Rich did with her Global Good Fund. Seize a small opportunity that seems right to you.
- **Find your why.** Listen to your heart, tap into your passion, and find your purpose.
- **Put others first.** Realize that significance comes from helping others and making their lives better.
- **Add value to others in your sweet spot.** Begin adding value to others using the things you naturally do well, and keep fine-tuning your efforts until it aligns with your sweet spot.

If you do those things, then you'll be ready to take the next important step, which is to begin working together with other like-minded and like-valued people who also want to make a difference. And that is the subject of the next section of the book.

# Intentional Application:
# Add Value to Others from Your
# Sweet Spot

## What Do You Have to Offer?

Examine your life from the perspectives outlined in the chapter:

- *Look backward—what have I been given?* What unique experiences and resulting insights can you use to add value to others?
- *Look inward—what do I have to give?* What talents, strengths, and skills do you possess that you can use to add value to others?
- *Look outward—what can I do?* What can you do *daily* to add value to others?

Write your answers to these questions. Then become determined to leverage what you have for others *every day*.

## What Do You *Feel* You Were Made to Do?

Another way to find your sweet spot for adding value to others is to pay attention to what you feel. When I add value to people by communicating with them, especially on the subject of leadership, it resonates within me.

What resonates within you? When do you possess the sense that you were made to do a particular thing? If you know the answer to that question, fantastic. However, if you can't immediately answer it, then you need to do some exploring.

Take time to brainstorm any and every moment in your life when you *felt* you were doing what you were meant to do. Write down each of those moments, what you were doing, and what exactly resonated in you. Then spend time reflecting on them until you can see a pattern or otherwise make some sense of it.

# WITH PEOPLE WHO MAKE A DIFFERENCE

# 7

## Connect with Like-Minded People

It is a fact that no person can achieve significance alone. It's never been done, nor will it ever be. I learned this in Lancaster, but the idea didn't really take full form for me until I wrote about it in *The 17 Indisputable Laws of Teamwork*. It was in that book that I identified the Law of Significance, which states that one is too small a number to achieve greatness.

People try to achieve great things by themselves mainly because of the size of their ego, their level of insecurity, their temperament, or simple naïveté. But it can't be done. That was a painful lesson I only needed to be taught once as a young leader. You may be able to achieve some degree of success by yourself, though even that is difficult. But it is impossible to live a life that matters and find significance without other people.

## Attracting People to a Cause

I have always been keenly aware that I have the kind of personality that attracts people to me and to whatever I'm excited about. The authors of *StrengthsFinder* call this "woo." While I was at Lancaster, I used this ability heavily. In fact, as soon as I realized that I needed to make a difference *with* people to achieve significance—instead of trying to make a difference *for* people—I started recruiting everybody I could to partner with me. I immediately began asking others to join my team. I became an Uncle Sam of significance. Everywhere I went, I pointed to everyone I saw and said, "I Want You."

In those days, I had dreams of being a positive influencer in our small town of Lancaster, Ohio. I wanted to build a large auditorium to house our growing congregation. I needed to start social programs to help people in need. I had a great desire to host leadership conferences to help others lead more successfully. My dreams were bigger than me, but they certainly weren't out of reach. True significance will always be bigger than the person with the dream. That's why it requires a team of people working together to achieve it.

I began to share my dream with anyone and everyone to see what it did to them. Whenever I spoke, I talked about my dream. If someone stopped me on the street or at the mall, he heard about my dream. If somebody passed me in a hallway, she heard my dream. I was looking for people with a heart to make a difference and who could make things happen. I was developing a leadership track, believing that people who could produce results could always get the job done. That didn't mean I only recruited leaders, but I felt certain if people could make good things happen for themselves, they could make positive things happen for others. I believed that if you have the heart to make a difference, there is always an answer, but if you have a heart of indifference, there is never an answer.

> If you have the heart to make a difference, there is always an answer, but if you have a heart of indifference, there is never an answer.

As I spread the word about what I wanted to do and how I wanted to include others, many people joined me. I was passionate, and passion is contagious. And that's a good thing because it takes a lot more energy to do something for other people than for ourselves. The good news is that I was moving from *me* to *we* during this time. But I still had a lot to learn.

Many people eagerly climbed aboard the Maxwell train. I thought that was success. It took me a couple of years to figure out that the people who were joining me in the early days just wanted to come along for the ride. They liked my enthusiasm and energy, and they wanted to be close to me, but they didn't necessarily share the same passion I had for significance, for making a difference with others. They just wanted to hang out. They lacked the passion to make a difference, which meant they didn't have the same goal or purpose I did. We were on the same train but wanted to go in different directions.

At first I thought the problem was that they were on the *wrong* train. Instead of asking, "What can we do for others?" they were asking, "What can you do for me?" But then it dawned on me—they weren't on the wrong train. I had simply recruited the wrong people to get on board the train I wanted to take— the significance train. I should have checked their tickets. I should have shared the purpose of the journey I was taking before I said, "All aboard!"

This required another shift in my thinking. I had to stop the proverbial train and allow everyone who wasn't holding a significance ticket to get off. Then I had to proactively go out and attract the *right* people and begin the journey again.

So who were the right people? They were people who were making a difference in the lives of others, not just people who wanted to hang out with those who were making a difference. There is a big difference between the two. When you surround yourself with people who really want to make a difference, people who crave and are willing to work toward significance, there is always a way to make a difference, no matter the obstacles.

How was I going to connect with these people? I realized I needed to have a clearer picture of what I was trying to accomplish. I needed to get clarity for myself and for my cause. Once I got that, I could declare it to others and see how they would respond.

## Articulating a Dream

So I took the next six months to carefully construct a statement describing what I was seeking. It became my own version of "I Have a Dream," inspired by the speech of the great Martin Luther King Jr. Certainly my version was not as good as his—how could it be? But it was the best I could make it. It took me *at least* fifty drafts before I finally got it to be a version I could live with. It was my first attempt at writing a vision statement that I thought would attract the right kind of people into my world, people who shared my passion to make a difference for others, and it stuck for a very long time.

On the next page is what I wrote:

## I Have a Dream

History tells us that in every age there comes a time when leaders must come forth to meet the needs of the hour. Therefore, there is no potential leader who does not have an opportunity to better mankind. Those around him also have the same privilege. Fortunately, I believe that God has surrounded me with those who will accept the challenge of this hour.

My dream allows me to...

1. Give up at any moment all that I am in order to receive all that I can become.
2. Sense the invisible so I can do the impossible.
3. Trust God's resources since the dream is bigger than all my abilities and acquaintances.
4. Continue when discouraged, for where there is no faith in the future, there is no power in the present.
5. Attract winners because big dreams draw big people.
6. See myself and my people in the future. Our dream is the promise of what we shall one day be.

Yes, I have a dream. It is greater than any of my gifts. It is as large as the world but it begins with one. Won't you join me?

I took what I wrote to a print shop and had it printed and laminated on five-by-seven-inch cards so that I could hand them out. I gave hundreds of cards to people. Any time I sensed that someone might be seeking significance, I gave him or her a card.

When I gave it to people, there was no pressure, no strings attached, and no cultish sales pitch. All I did was hand them a card and say, "Read this. If you want to join me, let me know." If they asked questions, I took no more than a couple of minutes to share my dream of significance with them. Every time someone reached out their hand, without realizing it, they were accepting a little piece of me into their lives—and that act alone was another small step toward intentional living. Hundreds and eventually thousands of people joined me.

It turned out that my "I Have a Dream" card was an important piece of my significance journey because it told people who I was, what I did, and what I wanted to accomplish. It was a tangible way to express what I felt, to put my ideas out there and quickly identify like-minded people who would want to join me.

Remember, after I figured out that I needed to consider who I was recruiting, I didn't give the card to just anyone. I only handed it to those I felt had the significance mindset. I used it selectively, and when I did, it was an easy way to say, "The ball is in your court." Those who weren't ready to get in the game with me may still be sitting in the bleachers, watching life from the sidelines. Happily though, the majority of those I chose to give the card to took that ball, looked me straight in the eyes, and said, "Count me in!" Now that's what I call getting in the game.

I intuitively knew that the way I wrote my dream card would appeal to the right people because the wording was deliberate and meant to be an intentional eliminator. Why? Because my "I Have a Dream" was really a challenge. You see, great vision is a separator: People who migrated toward the vision wanted significance. Those who backed away from it wanted something else, which was fine. I didn't want to partner with people who were choosing to live without passion, without significance, and without intentionality.

I continued to print these cards and hand them out for two years. And soon the vision began to catch fire. I knew something special was happening when reactions started to change from, "Sure, I'll take this card," to, "Do you mind if I keep this?" I never once asked anyone to join me. I just gave out the cards and said, "Think about it. Get back to me." I left the decision in their hands. And I was attracting the exact people I'd been looking for.

Because I am a person of faith, I think I should tell you that it was during this season that I also began to ask God every day to send me people who wanted to make a difference. And He answered those prayers. When people would show up and introduce themselves to me, I would say to myself, "He brought me another one." I met sharp people who were going to make a difference, and I was grateful.

It's hard to express my gratitude to God for these people and how much I appreciate them. But to help you understand, I'm going to jump ahead in my own personal story and tell you about something I did in 1995 after I resigned from Skyline, my church in California.

After I had made the announcement that I was leaving but before the day I stepped down, I sent out invitations to six hundred people asking them to join me for a closing banquet. I'm sure they all thought it was a going-away dinner for me. I didn't tell them why they were really being invited that night. Regardless of the reason, nearly everyone showed up.

That evening I explained why I wanted them to be there. "None of you know this," I said, "but for years, I've prayed that God would give me people who wanted to make a difference with me. And he gave me each of you."

A hush fell across the room that I will never forget.

I visited every individual table that night and spent hours reminding each person where I had met him or her for the first time. It was one of those rare times in life that I knew how special the moment was while it was happening. And I somehow understood that it would never happen again for any of us who were there.

Words can hardly honor the depth of emotion that swelled in the room. It filled my heart with blessed joy. Almost every one of us wept because we all understood God had put a plan in motion so much bigger than any of us. It was the ultimate culmination of my decades-long search for people who would join me in the journey of significance.

Let me stop a moment and say something important to you. You don't have to be a world-class leader to connect with like-minded people to make a difference. You don't have to be a Martin Luther King Jr. or a Mother Teresa or a Nelson Mandela to be part of something significant. I hope you know that. In fact, you don't have to be a leader at all. Most people who make a difference don't have any kind of formal leadership position. They're just intentional— whether they are leading the team, working as part of the team, or supporting the team.

If you want to make a difference with people, you just need to find like-minded people who share common goals for doing something significant. You just need to want to make a difference together and then do it!

## Factors That Connect People of Significance

My wish for you is that you someday experience the same feeling that I felt at that closing banquet. I want you to connect with people who will go with you on your significance journey. I want you to work with like-minded people. And I believe you can.

To help you with that, allow me to show you nine factors that attract people of significance to one another. These observations are based on my version of "I Have a Dream." To explain how this works, I'll break what I wrote for my card into sections and explain each of them in turn. They will help you as you seek like-minded people in search of significance.

### 1. The Opportunity Factor

*History tells us that in every age there comes a time when leaders must come forth to meet the needs of the hour. Therefore, there is no potential leader who does*

*not have an opportunity to better mankind. Those*
*around him also have the same privilege.*

Significant acts almost always occur in response to opportunities. That was the case in 2013 when leaders from EQUIP and I had the chance to pursue a transformation initiative in the country of Guatemala by teaching people values. After we connected with leaders throughout the country, including in the government, we were asked to train nineteen thousand people in one week.

What a cause. What an opportunity. What a challenge! That would be a Herculean task for anyone to undertake.

How would we ever grasp such an opportunity? We'd partner with other like-minded people. I appealed to coaches from the John Maxwell Team, and nearly two hundred of them volunteered their time, flew down to Guatemala City, and paid all their own expenses to train Guatemalan leaders in how to facilitate roundtables.

These coaches really seized the moment and made a difference in the lives of many people, because the nineteen thousand people they trained went on to lead nearly two hundred thousand people in values roundtables. But the greatest difference occurred *within them*. They went to Guatemala to change others, but came back changed. They tasted significance, and once you taste significance, success will never again satisfy you.

What opportunities do you see? Do you see a way to connect others to significance? Or is someone inviting you to join him or her in doing something significant? If you see it, seize it. What you say yes to shapes your life. Sometimes the smallest step in the right direction ends up being the biggest step in your life. Tiptoe if you must, but take that first important step.

> Sometimes the smallest step in the right direction ends up being the biggest step in your life.

*Question: What opportunity do you see right now to make a difference?*

## 2. The Belief Factor

*Fortunately, I believe that God has surrounded me with those who will accept the challenge of this hour.*

As I've already told you, if you don't believe in God, I don't have any desire to push my personal beliefs or faith on you. I place no judgment on anyone. That being said, I know without a doubt that every day since I started asking God to bring me people who desired significance, He has been sending them into

my life so that we could make a difference together.
And God continues to send them.

A few weeks ago I was in an office supply store
talking to the clerk. A gentleman walked up to me
and said, "I recognize that voice." I smiled and spent
three minutes getting acquainted with this kind
stranger, whose name was Troy. At the end of our
brief conversation, he invited Margaret and me to
dinner the next evening.

Then the following morning I received this text
from Troy:

> I know you are busy with your book. But I felt I
> needed to tell you this before tonight's dinner. The
> Lord woke me up last night and I asked Him if He
> wanted to tell me something. He told me to tell you
> that I am the one you have been praying about. I have
> no idea what it means and will not speculate. I just had
> to be obedient in sharing it with you.

Even before he sent the text, I already knew. He
was someone who wanted to make a difference, and
God had put him in my path.

That night Margaret and I met Troy and his wife,
Randi, for dinner. I made a conscious decision ahead
of time that I would take the conversation as far as
he wanted it to go. I didn't want to be presump-
tive or pushy. I wanted Troy to know our meeting

wasn't by chance. I told him these kinds of meetings happen to me often. Why? Because I ask God for them.

Whenever God sends another person to me who wants to make a difference, and he or she wants to meet with me, I don't go in expecting anything. I am not trying to lead anyone's life or take control. I don't try to use spiritual leverage on them. I know I'm just there to listen and share my story of intentionality and significance. I rarely spend more than fifteen minutes talking about such things before suggesting we move on to other topics.

That night the four of us had a nice dinner. Troy and I have sporadically kept in touch since then. He is excited to become a part of the work I am doing. He sees himself as a trainee in our leadership program so he can learn how to grow his businesses. He also wants to move into a mentoring role someday. As a result of a "chance" meeting in an office supply store that really wasn't by chance, Troy is now walking on his own road of significance.

You don't have to believe in God to believe that like-minded people will come into your life when you have it in your heart to do something significant. Do you believe that? Do you believe others want to connect with you to make a difference? When someone who wants to make a difference comes across your path, do you recognize him or her? Do you believe enough in that person to connect with him or her and to start thinking about what you might do together to make a difference? Belief is essential for significance. Without belief, you will have a very difficult time living intentionally and striving for significance.

*Question: Do you believe people are coming to you to help you make a difference?*

## 3. The Possibility Factor

*My dream allows me to give up at any moment all that I am in order to receive all that I can become.*

If you want to live a life of significance, you will have to give up some things. The pathway of possibility is filled with trade-offs. Why? Because there is no significance without sacrifice. But the good news is that as you trade one thing for another, you will be moving toward a better and more fulfilling way of life, whether making a difference means making the decision to start a family or making radical changes to your everyday life.

Each of us is faced with moments in life where we are forced to stop, reflect, and consider our options. Nearly every choice is a trade-off, and we start making them early in life. Will we watch television shows or play outside? Will we play in high school or work to get good grades? Will we take a job when we finish high school to make some money right away, or will we go to college? When we graduate, will we take the job that pays more money or will we choose the one that will give us better experience?

The trade-offs we make impact, well, everything. And know this: the more successful you are, the greater and more challenging the trade-offs will be that you have to make.

As I look at my long career, all I see is a long series of trade-offs. The majority of times I changed positions, I took a pay cut. But every time I transitioned to a situation where I had greater opportunities. After making the biggest transition of my career, which I'll tell you about in the next chapter, I looked back at all of the trade-offs I'd made, and wrote a lesson about it. I used it to encourage leaders to reach for their greater possibilities. Here are the trade-offs I recommended they make:

- Trade Affirmation for Accomplishment.
- Trade Security for Significance.
- Trade Financial Gain for Future Potential.
- Trade Immediate Pleasure for Personal Growth.
- Trade Exploration for Focus.
- Trade Quantity of Life for Quality of Life.

- Trade Acceptable for Excellent.
- Trade Addition for Multiplication.
- Trade the First Half for the Second Half.

If you want to live a life that matters, you will have to make trade-offs. They are required in our significance journey. And as I already said, they become harder as we become more successful. But know this: trade-offs never leave you the same. And if you trade up for significance over serving yourself, those changes will always be for the better.

*Question: What are you willing to give up to make a difference?*

## 4. The Faith Factor

*My dream allows me to sense the invisible so I can do the impossible. Trust God's resources...*

Again, I frame this in the context of my faith, but the issue here is really about fear. Almost everything you and I want is on the other side of fear. How do you handle that? How do you get beyond your fears?

For me it's a faith issue. I try to leave everything in God's hands, and I usually see God's hand in everything. I don't believe God gives me a dream to frustrate me. He gives me a dream to be fulfilled.

Do you want to know something amazing? Fear is the most prevalent reason why people stop. Faith is what makes people start. Fear is the key that locks the door to the resources. Faith is the key that opens that door.

> **Fear is the most prevalent reason why people stop. Faith is what makes people start.**

When your dream of significance is right, it should increase your faith. You should believe your dream *can* be accomplished. Faith should help you see the invisible and do the impossible. It should help release the resources you need. Even if you have a different kind of dream from mine, I believe you can trust God's resources.

The faith factor encourages me to start walking and to believe the resources will come to me as I walk. I know they will not come if I sit still. If I stop, the resources stop. Resources come to us when we are on our missions, when we are fulfilling our callings.

The lesson I teach most often on faith is this: feed your faith and starve your fear. To do that you must give your faith more energy than your fear. You can't reduce fear by thinking about it. You reduce it by taking action away from it. How? By moving toward faith.

Before I move on, let me say this to you just in case you happen to be a person of faith. Most people ask

God for knowledge first, and then move. God wants us to move first and then He gives us knowledge. God asked Moses to go back to Egypt. Moses didn't understand why. And he didn't want to go. But after he did go back to Egypt, he understood what God was doing. The biggest mistake people of faith make is feeling God owes them an explanation. God owes us nothing.

The book of Job is a great piece of literature and a terrific example of the faith factor. If you're familiar with the story, you understand that Job suffers terrible tragedy, losing his children, his possessions, and his health. Job continuously asks, "Why?" yet God never answers his question. Instead God takes him through the process. Why? Because it's all about the process. Philip Yancey says, "We're concerned with how things turn out; God seems more concerned with how we turn out." Our acting on faith is often how God grows us.

Faith does not make things easy, but it makes things possible because it puts everything, including fear, into the right perspective. So if you want to learn, to grow, to achieve your dreams of significance and to make a difference, have faith.

*Question: Is my faith greater than my fear?*

## 5. The Challenge Factor

*...the dream is bigger than all my abilities and acquaintances.*

Sometimes I think there are no great men or women. There are just great challenges that ordinary people like you and me are willing to tackle. Why do I say that? Because nothing separates passionate people from passive people like a call to step up. Whenever I invite others to join me in doing something big by casting a vision of significance, I realize that some people will respond positively to it and others will run from it.

That must have been true when Christopher Columbus was looking for sailors in preparation for his first voyage west. A few years ago I came across the words that he supposedly posted when looking for his crew. I'm sure it's apocryphal, but I love it just the same:

### *Wanted*
*Bold, brave adventurous souls to accompany me on an exciting voyage.*

*Final destination? Home.*

*First few stops? Uncertain, but probably off the maps and charts.*

*Length of journey? Unknown.*
*Hazards and dangers? Many.*
*Cost to you? Your time, money, and maybe your life itself.*
*Rewards? God alone knows but God alone decides.*
*Opportunity? The one of a lifetime!*
*Will you come with me?*
       *—Christopher Columbus, written in 1491*

At age sixty-eight, I feel more challenged to make a difference than at any other time in my life. It is my passion to raise up people as intentional leaders so that they will rise up and become transformational leaders. As I have studied movements of transformation I have endeavored to define what a transformational leader looks like. I believe transformational leaders influence people to think, speak, and act in such a way that it makes a positive difference in their lives and in the lives of others. It's my dream—and my challenge—to develop transformational leaders. It's much easier to define one than it is to develop one. However, I have accepted the challenge.

My hope is that this book will help you to move in this direction—to become intentional in making a difference, and to help take others there as well. If you and I do that and help others to do the same, we can help transform individuals and communities.

*Question: Are you challenged to stretch to significance?*

## 6. The Attitude Factor

*My dream allows me to continue when discouraged, for where there is no faith in the future, there is no power in the present.*

I've always been impressed by the leadership of Martin Luther King Jr. He was able to inspire so many people to perform significant acts during his relatively short lifetime. It led to a movement that created positive change for America. King once said, "The biggest job in getting any movement off the ground is to keep together the people who form it." I believe a big part of his success in doing that came from his attitude. He never seemed to lose hope. He kept believing in the change he was working toward, up to the very end of his life.

When I lived in Atlanta, I had the privilege of meeting numerous people who both marched with Dr. King and were jailed with him. They overcame a lot to make a difference for those who came behind them. And while King was alive, he kept them together. He helped people to keep their attitudes like his.

I've often wondered why so many good people stop doing good things in their lives. I've concluded that people lose energy not because the work they do is hard, but because they forget why they started doing it in the first place. They lose their *why* and as a result, they lose their way. When their attitudes slip, so do their efforts.

I believe most people who try to make a difference start out with the right motives and attitudes. As a result, the people they help gain a tremendous amount from them. But what often starts to occur is a shift in thinking, from *I want to help people* to *I want people to help me.* This is especially destructive when this shift occurs in the leaders. The moment that transition in attitude takes place, the leaders' motives change. Instead of enlisting people to whom they can add value and who will join them in adding value to others, the leaders want to attract people who can add value to *themselves.*

When people are motivated by personal advantage, they've lost their way. As a result, they get off track and they can no longer make a difference. When you stop loving people, you stop serving them well. If you're wondering, *Why aren't others serving me?* it becomes a source of discontent. And if you're a leader, you forfeit your leadership effectiveness.

Attitude so often is the difference maker. I had a friend who once said to me, "When life is sweet, say thank you and celebrate. When life is bitter, say thank you and grow." That's a great attitude. And it's the kind of attitude required to make a difference and connect with other difference makers.

And let me say one more thing about attitude. It's easy to have a good attitude when life is good. The time a positive attitude really counts is when things are going badly. We don't always choose what happens to us, but we can always determine how we respond. When we choose the right attitude even when things are going wrong, that is highly attractive and appealing to the people who partner with us.

*Question: Is your attitude an asset or liability?*

## 7. The Winning Factor

*My dream allows me to attract winners because big dreams draw big people.*

When I wrote the above sentence for my "I Have a Dream" card, I can remember how I felt. The dream that I possessed thrilled me, but it had not yet attracted many people who could help me achieve it. I wanted to connect with people motivated by significance who could make things happen. But I also wondered how such people might react to my invitation.

*Would they understand my dream?*

*Would my dream widen the gap between them and me?*

*Would they criticize it?*

When I looked at the people I knew, I was tempted to keep my dream to myself. Sharing a dream of significance is a risk. It can invite ridicule or rejection. But I also knew that if I wanted to achieve the goal of making a difference, I had to connect with good people so that we could work together. So I gathered my courage, took a leap of faith, and made the decision to tell others.

The responses I received were varied and interesting. Most people fell into one of three categories: survival, success, and significance. People interested only in survival hid. They wanted no part of my vision. Some people who were seeking success bought in. But the ones who most readily connected were those who wanted significance. Big dreams draw people with potential who want to jump in the deep end, way over their heads, and learn to swim.

> Dreams often come one size too big so that we can grow into them.

Another discovery I made while sharing my dream was surprisingly delightful. Dreams often come one size too big so that we can grow into them. It's like when I was a child and my parents always bought my shoes one half size too big. They would say, "John, you're growing. You're becoming a young man. You will grow into these in no time."

That's what I now say to people when they first put on their significance shoes. They may feel a little too big for you at the moment, but don't worry. As you start taking steps, you will grow into them and become the significant person you were created to be.

Are you taking the risk of sharing your dreams of significance with others? And are talented, successful, motivated people connecting with you so that you can try to achieve those dreams together? You need those winning kinds of people to make a difference. And you need to *be* one of those winners yourself!

When it comes to significance, I still feel like I'm wearing shoes that are too big and I need to grow into them. I'm still in over my head and trying to swim. And that's good. I'm getting older in years, but younger in my dreams. That's what makes me love this journey I'm on.

*Question: Are you connecting with winners to achieve significance?*

## 8. The Promise Factor

*My dream allows me to see myself and my people in the future. Our dream is the promise of what we shall one day be.*

When I wrote this phrase, I truly believed a worthy dream contained a promise of its fulfillment. But that was a naïve mistake. I had made the same mistake most people make about dreams. I thought, *if you believe it, you can achieve it.* But that's not always true. A dream requires a partner: commitment.

Dreams are free. However, the journey to fulfill them isn't. You have to work for your dream. Your dream doesn't work for you. You have to work with the dream and for the dream. The dream is a *promise* of what you can be, but *commitment* is the reality of what you will become. What starts as a promise ends as a commitment.

*Question: Have you committed to a path with great promise for you and others?*

## 9. The Invitation Factor

*Yes, I have a dream. It is greater than any of my gifts. It's as large as the world but it begins with one. Won't you join me?*

We all have a certain amount of luck in our lives, but the best luck is what I like to call "who luck." Why? Because *who* you connect with matters the most. The "who luck" in your life can be either good or bad, depending on who joins you. I'm sure you know that instinctively. Haven't you met people who worked with you who made it easier for both of you to make a difference? And haven't you also connected with people you later wished you'd never met— because they hindered your ability to make a difference? I have.

All my life I've looked for ways to connect with others, as a church leader, a business leader, and a communicator. But you don't have to be a leader to invite people to something of significance. You just need to be committed to your cause and open to working with others to achieve it. In fact, if you think leadership is getting people to follow you, you may be a good leader. But if you think leadership is getting people to follow a great cause, you have the potential to be a great leader. If your *why* is big enough to excite you, then, as you share it, it will excite others— especially those who share your passion and dream. The size of your *why* will determine the size of your response.

*Question: Are you ready to start inviting others to join you in living a life that matters?*

## A Heart for Veterans

Recently I read a story about someone who began making a difference in the lives of others after he felt compelled to do what he thought was right. That action led him down a pathway of significance that he didn't expect. His name is Zach Fike. He is an officer in the Army National Guard and a collector of antiques. His journey began when his mother, Joyce, bought him a gift for Christmas in 2009. It was a Purple Heart medal she had found in an antique store. Joyce thought her son would add the medal to his collection.

But the moment Zach saw it and read the name engraved on it, Corrado Piccoli, something stirred within him. Military service ran in the blood of Zach's family. Joyce was a drill instructor. Zach's father had served as a command sergeant major. He had relatives who had served in the Revolutionary War, the War of 1812, the Civil War, World War I, World War II, and Vietnam.

"I knew that medal didn't belong to me," says Zach. "And it sent me on a journey to find the family."[21]

As it turned out, he couldn't do that right away, because he was deployed to Afghanistan. But after he got back, he tracked down the relatives of Piccoli, who had been killed in action in France during World War II. In a ceremony honoring Piccoli,

Zach returned the medal to Piccoli's sister, Adeline Rockko, who was eighty-seven.[22]

"I saw something very special happen around that return," Zach says. "After the serviceman's death, the family kind of went on in their own direction. They all separated. Because of this medal return I saw a family come together again. And they had their first-ever family reunion sixty-five years [after Piccoli's death]."[23]

That inspired Zach to begin looking for other lost or stolen Purple Hearts that he could return to their rightful owners or their surviving families. When he'd find one, he'd have it professionally mounted in a shadow box, often with other medals the veteran had earned, and he would present them at a ceremony. Word began to spread about what he was doing. People began sending Purple Hearts they'd found. And others told him that they were seeking Purple Hearts that had been lost. Eventually, Zach started a nonprofit organization called Purple Hearts Reunited to make it easier for people to support the effort and be a part of it. So far, Zach has returned more than two hundred medals.

After Zach began doing this, he received a Purple Heart himself after being injured in a rocket attack. But that's not what motivates him. He wants to make a difference.

"[For] a lot of these families, it's closure," he says about the Purple Heart medals he returns. "It's the only tangible thing that the families received after their loved one died. It's something you can touch, that you can hold, that you can look at. And that's all they have of him. It's probably the most important thing in their lives."[24]

## The Making of a Movement

Right now are you only dreaming about making a difference, or are you actually doing things to connect with people who can join you on the significance journey? Movements don't begin with the masses— they always start with one, and then they attract others to themselves and their causes. That was the case in the antiapartheid movement in South Africa. In 1941, this is what South African antiapartheid activist Walter Sisulu wrote about Nelson Mandela: "We wanted to be a mass movement and then one day a mass leader walked into the office."

Anyone on the planet today can start a movement. You can, I can, and even the guy or gal sitting next to you on the plane, bus, or subway can. Movements are about mobilizing people to get behind a shared purpose. There is great power in starting movements because they can change the way people think, believe, and even live. They can start out with just a small group of people who believe in something passionately, and they can end up changing the culture, if not the world.

Today I have another dream. I want to see people become intentional in their living. I want to see them become transformational leaders who influence others to think, speak, and act in such a way that it makes a positive difference. Will it become a movement? I don't know. I have no control over that. I only have control over myself. I know that it has to start with me, and I feel moved to share it with you.

This book is my invitation for you to join me. I want you to embrace these ideas, and for the story of your life to change, as mine has. I want you to take action to make a positive difference in the lives of others. I want you to connect with others and achieve significance. And my hope, someday, is to hear a million stories of changed lives because people like you and me tried to make a difference for others.

If you join me in my dream, maybe together we can help create a world of intentional living where people think of others before themselves, where adding value to others is a priority, where financial gain is secondary to future potential, and where your self-worth is strengthened by acts of significance every day. It's my dream. I hope one day it becomes our reality. But it can come to be only if we connect with others and work together.

# Intentional Application:
# Connect with Like-Minded People

## What Is Your Dream?

Most people who would like to do something significant have ideas and intentions, but they rarely have specific, vivid pictures of their dreams written out. That lack of clarity makes it more difficult for them to achieve their dreams—and to connect with other like-minded people who would be interested in partnering with them to accomplish those dreams.

Take some time to write out your dream. It can contain your principles, as mine did. It can contain specifics, as Martin Luther King Jr.'s did. It can be a poem, a story, a list. Make it your own, but be sure to *write it down*. You may be able to write it in a sitting. Or it may take you months, as it did me. That's not important. The process of writing it forces you to clarify your thinking and know what you want. And having it written gives you a record of your hopes and aspirations. Once it's done, you can decide whom to share it with.

## Start Connecting with Others to Find Like-Minded People

I know it may seem risky and it may make you feel vulnerable, but you need to start telling others about your dream for making a difference. Begin sharing it with people who will encourage you, whether or not they are likely to join you. Then widen your circle. Begin telling people whom you believe to be like-minded, and see where it leads.

# 8

## Partner with Like-Valued People

In 1987, I turned forty. I saw this birthday as a major milestone, so I approached it as an athlete would halftime. I saw it as an opportunity to check the scoreboard of my life, assess my performance, analyze my deficiencies, and begin making adjustments before going back out on the field to play my second half. In the eyes of others, I had accomplished some major achievements. But when I stopped to examine my life, I was not satisfied. I felt there was something greater I wasn't doing.

### The Next Steps in My Journey

To help you understand this, I need to catch you up on my story and tell you what I was doing during the ten years before my fortieth birthday. Margaret and I left Lancaster in 1979. Why would we leave people we loved, a church where we were making a difference, and an area where we felt at home? That's a fair question.

We were highly successful in Lancaster, but I began to want to do more. And I started to wonder if the leadership principles I was developing and the values I was embracing could be used in organizations I wasn't leading myself. In other words, I wondered if I could make a difference beyond my personal reach, through other leaders I trained in other parts of the country. Could I make a more significant impact?

I got a chance to test that idea when I was offered a position with another ministry organization at their national office. The new position would allow me to spend all of my time training pastors in churches around the country who were part of that organization. Margaret and I packed up Elizabeth and Joel, our two young children, and we moved to central Indiana.

The good news was that I discovered that the leadership ideas I had developed in Hillham and Lancaster *did* transfer. They really worked for anyone who valued leadership and was willing to become a better leader. Every leader I worked with who put my principles into practice was more successful. But there was also a downside. I was limited in who I could help since I was allowed to work only with people in that one organization. I wanted to reach more people, and that made me realize that the best place for me to do that was as the pastor of a local church. When I got the invitation to lead Skyline, a church in the San Diego area, I gladly accepted, and our family moved from Indiana to California. That was in 1981.

The first thing I started doing when we got there was to get the church, which had plateaued, growing again. The task of building a great church was familiar territory for me. I understood that world and knew what it would take. I rebuilt the staff, changed how we did things, and found creative ways to reach out into the community. It wasn't long before Skyline was recognized as one of the most influential churches in America by Elmer Towns, a church growth expert and college professor whom I admired and who became a good friend.

In the early eighties, I also started teaching leadership conferences outside of the church. When I took the position at Skyline, the board understood that I wanted to add value to other leaders, and they agreed to give me the flexibility to do that. When I was invited to start speaking for a training organization, I chose to teach R-E-A-L, the four things every person needs to be successful: relationships, equipping, attitude, and leadership.

Before long, I realized I wanted to emphasize leadership more in my communication, so I created a company called INJOY and started hosting my own conferences. To say that I believed big but started small would be an understatement. The first leadership conference I hosted myself was in Kansas City, Missouri. Only fourteen people signed up for it, and I stood to lose a couple thousand dollars if I went through with it. A friend told me doing it would be a bad business decision. But I could see that it would be a good *significance* decision, so I did it anyway.

That was the first of what became many dozens of conferences I ended up holding. Eventually hundreds and then thousands would attend and learn how to become better leaders. I wouldn't have described it this way at that time, but what I was really teaching leaders was intentional living.

At a small conference in a Holiday Inn in Jackson, Mississippi, a group of leaders told me that they were grateful for what I had taught them during the conference, but they wanted ongoing training. I wasn't sure what to do, but I wanted to help them. I could tell they wanted to make a difference. Have you ever been in a situation like that, where you felt compelled to do something, but you weren't sure how to make it happen?

Then I had a thought. I asked, "If I created a one-hour training tape every month, would you sign up for it as a subscription?" They said yes, so I passed a legal pad around the room to get their information. All thirty-five attendees signed up for it. That's how my monthly leadership tape club was born. That small list of people eventually exploded into more than fifteen thousand subscribers, with each tape being listened to by an average of five people. I was thrilled, because I was adding value to leaders, and they were multiplying that value to others.

## The Key to the Next Level

So by the time I turned forty, I had done a lot. When I looked at each of the things I had accomplished, I was happy with it. I felt what I had done had made a difference. So why was I feeling dissatisfied? Why wasn't I pleased? Why wasn't what I'd done enough? What had I missed?

That's when it hit me. I hadn't developed a team. There was no way I could be any more productive as an individual. For twenty years I'd found new and better ways to get more done. But I was at the limit. If I could develop a team, *we* could be more productive. Not only that, but we could do things *better* than I could do alone. I was living in *me* world, and I needed to be living in *we* world.

Had I been training leaders? Yes. Had I been including others in my significance journey? Yes. But had I been truly developing my team and partnering with them? No.

This became the birthday that challenged me to make major changes in the way I did things. The change in my thinking was huge. It was in the top half-dozen most important decisions I ever made. And it was *the* most important business decision of my life. I finally understood that life isn't made by what you can accomplish. It's made by what you can accomplish with others.

> Life isn't made by what you can accomplish. It's made by what you can accomplish with others.

From this point on in my life, every decision I made focused on developing others. And before long, it began compounding. Not only did I accomplish more, but my team accomplished more. I watched as they developed as people. And I discovered that I actually found greater joy in seeing them succeed than I did in succeeding myself. Wow! What a change that was for me.

I already mentioned to you that I regularly asked God to send me people who wanted to make a difference, and that I had thanked a group of six hundred of them before I left Skyline in 1995. This discovery when I was forty fueled my inclusion of these people into my world. It made me become more strategic and intentional in inviting people to join me in making a difference. Among those volunteers was Linda Eggers. There were many days when she partnered with me by volunteering to mail out tapes to leaders or pack boxes for conferences. In the midnineties, she became my executive assistant, and she still works in that capacity for me today. I can't imagine making a difference without her.

I also began to develop my staff in new ways. How could I travel often to train and develop other leaders yet still lead the church effectively? By developing great leaders who could lead without me. I partnered with Dan Reiland, who became my executive pastor, Steve Babby, who oversaw finances, and Tim Elmore, who did research and developed sermon outlines that he and I both taught. Every key person I partnered with shared the same values I did. But each had his or her own personality and skill set that contributed to the bigger vision to make a difference.

Out of this discovery came what later became the Law of the Inner Circle in *The 21 Irrefutable Laws of Leadership*. It states, "A leader's potential is determined by those closest to him." The reason I have been successful in the twenty-eight years since my fortieth birthday is that I understand this law, and every decision I've made since then has been based on finding like-valued people, developing their potential, and partnering with them to accomplish a shared vision.

## The Power of Partnership

Partnership with like-valued people is powerful. Perhaps the best way for me to explain it is to recount a conversation I had not long ago with a small group of leaders from Latin America. The eighteen men and women I was meeting with collectively had forty-five to fifty million people under their leadership. Although each of them was already extremely successful, none was hitting 100 percent of his or her capacity. By my estimation, almost every person in the room was averaging somewhere between 75 and 80 percent. My goal that day was to show them how to move up to the next level of impact.

When I asked the group their thoughts on how to make that happen, every answer they gave would have yielded only a very modest increase in their effectiveness—their best idea adding perhaps at most a 5 percent increase.

This was a sophisticated group of achievers, yet they didn't give the answer that I knew was the key. I believed that if they'd been aware of the answer, they would have already been practicing it. I could sense that they were getting restless, so I finally gave them the solution. "Partnerships," I said.

The room fell silent. It wasn't at all what they were expecting. But they got it immediately. We went on to have a great discussion of partnership and to trade ideas about potential partners.

Here's the most important thing to know about partnerships and alliances—to be effective, they must be made with like-minded, but more important, *like-valued* people. If you aren't connecting and partnering with people who share your dream *and* values, you have no shot at making these partnerships work.

Having the right partners will help you gain momentum and build your dream into something bigger. There's great strength in numbers. As the old adage says, two heads are better than one. Partnering with a community of like-valued people will help you multiply whatever dream you have of making a difference.

A community helps us go farther, and when it's a community of talented, like-valued, complementary people, we can actually go faster, too. Great partnerships make you better than you are, multiply your value, enable you to do what you do best, allow you to help others do their best, give you more time, provide you with companionship, help you fulfill the desires of your heart, and compound your vision and effort.

The moment you partner with somebody, you tap into something you've never had access to before. You gain their knowledge, experience, influence, and potential. When you are already achieving at a highly effective level, you don't gain a great increase by getting significantly better yourself. You gain it by partnering or connecting with other good people who bring something different to the table. And that makes you better. If the partnerships you make are with like-valued people, there's no limit to the difference you can make!

Many things can bring people together in the short term: passion, opportunity, urgency, convenience. However, if a partnership is to last over the long haul, there must be shared values. When people's values are different, there will inevitably be a parting of the ways.

It's important to know what you're looking for when it comes to shared values. Most people miss opportunities in life, not because the opportunity wasn't there, but because they didn't have a clue what it looked like when it arrived. They never took the time to figure out what they were looking for. It's all about intentionality. You have to know what you're looking for if you want to find it.

> Most people miss opportunities in life, not because the opportunity wasn't there, but because they didn't have a clue what it looked like when it arrived.

## Finding the Right Partners

Early in my career, I had no clear picture of who I was looking for—not when I entered the pastorate and not when I entered the business world. When I got started in my business life, I made some decisions to hire people who weren't the right fit. I had a blind spot when it came to people. I thought the best of everyone and couldn't always see people for who they really were. Despite those in my inner circle warning me and cautioning me, I always wanted to give people the benefit of the doubt. That got me into trouble more than once.

Since the picture of who I needed wasn't clear, I then allowed others to paint the picture for me. Invariably, they always painted *their* pictures. Then I discovered that the pictures they had painted of themselves had been greatly enhanced. They were like the glamour shots people take and then doctor in Photoshop.

How do I compensate for this now? I build in a 10 percent exaggeration factor.

The way this works became clear to me on the golf course. Bear with me for a moment, and you'll understand what I mean. Most golfers, you see, exaggerate their skills. It starts when they give their handicap. Unless they're sandbagging to try to win a bet, they typically overestimate their ability. Their best golf moment is on the first tee when they share their golf handicap. Then, they hit the ball and their true game shows up.

Golfers make the same mistake when they select a club during a round. Most golfers check their yardage, then select their club based on how far the ball would go if they hit a true shot with that club 100 percent of the time. Maybe one time they hit their 8 iron 150 yards with a pure swing. The rest of the time they hit it 135 yards. Their ball is lying at 150 yards, so what club do they choose? The 8 iron—the club they think they *should* hit 150 yards, not the club they actually *do* hit 150 yards with most of the time.

When I select a club for a shot, I subtract 10 percent of my distance from a perfect shot. In a round I may hit one 100 percent perfect shot, but I will hit twenty-five 90 percent shots. I select my clubs based upon what I most often do, not what I have done only once or twice in my whole life. Wrong club selection is the number one mistake of amateur golfers who hit the ball short of the hole.

When partnering with people, don't choose based on what they *say* they can do, or based on what they did *once*. Choose based on their regular behaviors. That's what tells you what their values are. Too often our choices are made by what we *could* or think we *should* do rather than what we *usually* do. We are all human, so we should give everyone the benefit of the doubt. But we also need to be realistic. We need to have a picture of what we're shooting for.

## The Twelve Qualities of Like-Valued People Who Seek Significance

When I wrote *The 21 Indispensable Qualities of a Leader*, it created a clear picture of what a leader looks like. If you're looking for leaders, look for those twenty-one qualities. Similarly, *The 17 Essential Qualities of a Team Player* drew a picture of what a good team member looks like. If you're looking for team players, look for those seventeen qualities in others.

But you're looking for people to join you on the path to your significance. To find them, what do you look for? The qualities of a like-valued person. You want to make sure people who join you share the same values of wanting to make their lives matter by doing significant acts for others. To help you to recognize these qualities, I've taken the time to identify what I look for in people when I am seeking to partner with them. I believe that this list will help you as you travel on your significance journey.

## 1. Like-Valued People Think of Others before Themselves

My favorite description of humility is this: people who are humble don't think less of themselves; they just think of themselves less. Maturity isn't growing older, nor getting wiser. It is developing the ability to see things from another person's point of view. When you combine humility with maturity you have the ideal person that I want to partner with, and probably the kind of like-valued person you want to look for, too. I'm drawn to people who understand that with one tiny exception, the world is composed of others.

## 2. Like-Valued People Think Bigger than Themselves

People who want to make a difference have expanded their worlds over the years from *me* to *we*. They have broken out of their selfish "what's in it for me" mindsets and have stretched beyond their own needs first. Their dreams now include helping others and reaching across fences to show that they are their brothers' keepers. They are grateful for the opportunity to serve their communities. They always approach others with a win/win mindset and always cross the finish line as relay team members, not single sprinters.

### 3. Like-Valued People Have a Passion That's Contagious

The people I want to partner with have a love for people and life that can be easily felt by everyone around them. When they walk into a room, their presence is palpably positive. Others are energized by their spirits, lifted by their love, and valued by their actions. To know them is to want to be around them. Their presence marks others and soon, everyone is inspired to live on a higher level so they too can pass on the joys of significant living to others.

### 4. Like-Valued People Have Complementary Gifts

Mother Teresa said, "I cannot do what you can do. You cannot do what I can do. Together we can do great things." Nothing is more rewarding than a common mission being achieved by people with complementary gifts working together in harmony. For years, the members of my inner circle have made me better because they are gifted differently than I am. Each person brings something unique to the table, and they are not afraid to share

> "I cannot do what you can do. You cannot do what I can do. Together we can do great things."
> —*Mother Teresa*

their knowledge or perspectives. Their presence adds value to everything I do. No one is the "total package." But if you put the right group of people together, you can create the total package.

When I wrote *The 21 Irrefutable Laws of Leadership*, it quickly became obvious that no one leader could perform all twenty-one laws with excellence. But soon leaders began developing teams who together could excel in all twenty-one laws. That's when they discovered that teamwork does make the dream work. There's an African proverb that says it best: "If you want to go fast, go alone. If you want to go far, go together." That's what like-minded significance partners do—help each other go far together.

## 5. Like-Valued People Connect and Provide Great Support

In the 1960s when I first began trying to make a difference, experienced leaders advised me as a young leader not to let anyone get too close to me. "Keep your distance," they said. I soon learned that was a mistake. You can't genuinely partner with people when you're not connected with them. Besides, today we live in a world of connections. There was a time when people could retreat to their own little castles, each surrounded by a moat to protect their privacy, and try to live in isolation. Today the moats are dried up.

Partners need to connect, and they need to support one another. Some of my closest friends are those who help me carry out my mission every day. Our worlds are forever linked. I often ask myself, "What would I do without them?" The answer is, "Not much."

## 6. Like-Valued People Show a Can-Do Creative Spirit about Challenges

If we want to fulfill our dreams and live out our *whys*, we need to partner with people who have a can-do spirit. Not everyone possesses that. When faced with obstacles, people have different responses. There are...

- **"I Can't" People:** They are convinced that they can't, so they won't and don't.
- **"I Don't Think I Can" People:** These people might be able to, but they talk themselves out of it. As a result they fulfill their words by not trying.
- **"Can I?" People:** These individuals allow their doubts to control their actions, which can lead to failure.
- **"How Can I?" People:** These people have already made the decision to tackle their tough

assignments. The only substantial question they struggle with is how they are going to do it.

This last group is my kind of people. Why? Because when we work together, *everything* is possible. It may take a while, but the vision will be accomplished.

## 7. Like-Valued People Expand Our Influence

For more than forty years I have taught that leadership is influence. During those years I have intentionally expanded my influence with others because I know it allows me to make a greater difference in the world. However, twenty years ago I made a great discovery. When I partner with like-valued people, I go from increasing to multiplying my influence.

Successful people understand that working hard at networking with other people is time well spent. It's the quickest and best way to find partners and opportunities to expand our influence.

## 8. Like-Valued People Are Activists

People who are willing to take a stand for what they believe in have an inherent bias toward action. There is no "ready, aim, aim, aim...fire" in their lives. If they err, it's on the side of "ready, fire, aim."

Activists don't merely accept their lives as they are; they lead their lives. They take things where they want them to go. They live their stories—100 percent. Nothing less is good enough for them. Every day they maximize opportunity and seize the chance to make their day a masterpiece.

### 9. Like-Valued People are Ladder Builders, Not Ladder Climbers

My friend Sam Chand, the speaker and consultant, taught me the difference between ladder climbers and ladder builders. He says, "We all start out life climbing our own ladders and living for ourselves. Over time, some people begin to shift from climbing to their own success, and they start building ladders for others to climb."

Sam has built a lot of ladders for others, including me. He's my kind of guy because he has dedicated his life to climbing with others toward a life of significance. If you want to make a difference, look for people like him.

### 10. Like-Valued People Are Head and Shoulders above the Crowd

The kinds of people I enjoy partnering with for significance are easy to find. Why do I say that?

Because they stand out from others. They take action when others won't. They add value to others every day. And their growth as human beings is dramatic as a result of intentionally making a difference in the lives of others. The only time you can't see them is when they're stooping down to help someone else.

My kinds of people want others to do better than they do, so that they too can rise higher and accomplish more. Metaphorically, they allow others to stand on their shoulders. They are record setters who want to help others break their own records. As you look for partners who will help you make a difference, search for those who stand out in a crowd.

## 11. Like-Valued People Provide Synergy That Gives a High Return

When you partner with the right person, it's like $1 + 1 = 3$. There is a synergy that comes when the right people are working together. It's similar to what happens when a group of horses work together. Maybe you've heard about that. For example, two horses can pull about nine thousand pounds together. How many pounds can four horses pull? Without synergy, you'd do the math and assume the answer is eighteen thousand pounds. That would be reasonable, but it would be wrong. Four horses working together can actually pull over thirty thousand pounds.

Synergy makes the whole greater than the simple sum of its parts. Its true meaning comes from the Greek word *synergia*, which means "working together." Think about all the positive possibilities when two or more things work together. Imagine playing the violin with just one hand. Add your other hand and you have the potential to become a virtuoso. What can you create with just flour? Not much. But if you add water and yeast, and then bake it, you can create bread.

When it comes to partnerships, synergy enables the group to outperform even its best individual members. That teamwork will produce an overall better result than if each person within the group was working toward the same goal individually. What can't be accomplished when there's synergy and commitment involved? United you can do much, much more!

## 12. Like-Valued People Make a Difference in Us

When I started partnering with other people, it was my intent that together we would make a difference for others. What surprised me was that the partnerships also made such a great difference for me. I discovered it is much more fun to do things together. But more important, I became a better person because of those who came alongside me.

As you seek out like-valued people to develop partnerships with, I need to let you know what the best foundation is for building a good partnership: similar capacity. Partnerships are lost more out of mismatched capacity than anything else. A solid partnership comes together because two people have something to offer each other, and what they give and receive are equally valued. It works like a scale. If one person is doing more giving than the other, then the partnership becomes unbalanced and it becomes strained. For the partnership to last, it has to come back into some kind of balance where the two feel the give-and-take works for both of them. And if the partnership is going to last, as it goes down the road and it grows, adapts, and evolves, both members must be able to change and adjust. If they don't, it will end. As long as each partner continues adding value to the other and as long as there is capacity on both sides, the partnership can blossom.

Most times when you enter into a partnership, you don't know in advance how it will go or if it will last. For it to have a chance, you have to spend a lot of connecting time with your partner, nurturing the relationship like any other. If you don't nurture that relationship, it's like any other living thing you ignore: it dies. Partnership starts with finding common ground and common goals. From there it builds from the relational to the inspirational.

And you have to remember that partnerships are more like movies than photographs. They change from moment to moment. Only time lets you know what's coming next. Capacity can't be predicted any more than trust can. But if you share intentionality, if you share vision, if you have common goals and a common purpose, if you're moving in the same direction, and if you are like-minded and like-valued, you've got a

> A strong partnership divides the effort and multiplies the effect.

pretty good shot at making the partnership work. A strong partnership divides the effort and multiplies the effect. And if both keep giving, it has a shot at lasting.

I know that you may have a cause or a passion project you're already actively involved in. Or perhaps you already possess the desire to start doing something good in your community. While my daily mission is to make a difference by adding value to leaders, yours might be raising money for the local homeless shelter or animal rescue. Maybe your dream is to help families by volunteering at a food bank. Maybe you want to tutor special-needs children. Whatever your passion is, think about how your effectiveness could be multiplied if you started connecting and partnering with the *right* people. Whatever difference you're able to make will be multiplied.

## Another Transition

I spent fourteen years leading Skyline, from 1981 to 1995. And I loved it. We made a positive impact on our community. We donated significant amounts of money to the county for projects every year. And we led many people to lives of significance. In addition, people came from all over to visit the church, attend services, and worship among the thousands of congregants. Wherever I traveled, people would say, "This is one of the most influential pastors in the country." In the eyes of many, I had reached the pinnacle of success as a pastor.

While I was appreciative of the opportunities I'd been given throughout the years, and was grateful to be included in the company of leaders that I viewed as better, faster, and smarter than I was, I had a sense that I could make an even greater impact. I felt I could be more significant by serving and adding value to people outside the church than I could if I remained in the pastorate.

I knew that meant making another transition. That's when I began to wrestle with the "greater than" concept. What must we give up in order to do something greater than what we're doing now?

I recognized I could no longer hold on to all I had if I wanted to move on, serve more people, and do bigger things. I knew it would be impossible to keep leading Skyline and help even more people outside the church at the same time. I couldn't do both with excellence.

This wouldn't be an easy decision. All my life I had been able to point to something tangible as a symbol of my success. I worried that if I left the church, I would no longer have that, and the loss of this aspect of my personal identity gave me great hesitancy about resigning. However, I knew it was time to reinvent myself and go toward my higher calling, where I knew I could serve others and make a difference.

Every time you make a big, potentially life-altering decision, there is going to be some sort of a trade-off. The more successful you are, the harder the trade-offs. If I was going to leave the church and everything I had worked so hard to achieve, I knew I needed to put my energy and focus on something big—something that mattered to me and that I valued even more.

## New Partnerships

So I tendered my resignation at Skyline, and I started to focus my attention on making a difference more broadly. I knew that I would continue to train leaders. During the fourteen years I had led leadership conferences, more and more businesspeople had begun showing up to learn from me, even though the conferences were designed primarily for church leaders. So I knew I would continue teaching leadership.

At this time I also put more focus on writing books. I wanted to make a difference in the lives of people I would never get to meet or who would not attend my conferences. I began partnering with Charlie Wetzel as my writer. Since then, he and I have written nearly seventy books together.

The second area where I put more energy was in helping other church leaders raise money for building projects. One of the things I had done not only at Skyline but also in Lancaster and Hillham was raise money to construct new buildings and relocate our growing congregations. I remember thinking to myself, *If I can raise millions of dollars for my church, what would happen if I started a company that could help churches and pastors all over America to do that?* I started another company and hired some good leaders I knew to become consultants to churches. I partnered with the consultants, who partnered with the churches. Together, we helped churches to raise $3 billion.

But perhaps the greatest partnership effort I made came when my brother Larry and I founded the nonprofit organization EQUIP. The seed for the idea was planted in 1985, when I was thirty-eight years old. I was coming home from a trip to Peru, where I had spent a week speaking to a group of American translators. They were a group of very smart and talented people, but they were consumed with their work. They were in leadership positions, and I spoke to them about improving their leadership skills, but they weren't especially responsive to my message, and, frankly, I was disgusted by their lack of interest in the help I was trying to offer them. They couldn't see beyond their pressing responsibilities to learn something new that would help them improve their leadership skills.

On the flight home, I turned to Margaret and said, "I don't want to speak in other countries anymore. In America I can use all of my tools to impart what I've learned. I can fall back on my sense of humor to teach my leadership principles and get a response from nearly any audience. Whenever I speak internationally, the response is slow at best because there are cultural differences. It's hard work. I don't need to work that hard! I think I'll stay home."

Margaret responded by asking, "Is there a need to raise up solid leaders around the world?"

"Of course," I replied.

"Do you believe that you can help them become better leaders?"

"Yes," I answered. "But it's a slow, laborious process and it's not what I like to do."

"John, God didn't give you your gifts for you to please yourself. He gave them to you to help others."

Wow! Those words hit me in the gut. The moment she said it, I knew she was right. I dropped the subject in our conversation, but I could not get rid of it in my mind. For the next several days I mentally and spiritually wrestled with the selfishness of my heart. I knew what I *should* do, and boy, was it at odds with what I *wanted* to do.

This wasn't going to be a situation where I could make a list of pros and cons and act on whichever column had more items listed. I knew the importance of the individual pros would have greater weight than the sheer number of cons. No matter how much I wanted to stay in my comfort zone, stay away from unfamiliar food, rely on my American humor, and stick with the relative ease of traveling within my own country, I had to face a decision.

When I did sit down with a legal pad in my favorite thinking chair, I listed on my con side of the list more than a dozen reasons why I didn't want to teach internationally. On the pro side, there were only two:

1. It was the right thing to do.
2. I couldn't ignore my true calling.

In the end, I knew that if I didn't follow through, the loser would be me. Why? Because I wouldn't be doing the one thing I had committed myself to—adding value to the lives of others. I had never put conditions on where people had to live when I made that commitment. If I wanted to reach my significance potential, I needed to be willing to put others first.

From that time, I began to accept more invitations to teach leadership outside of the United States. But the power of partnership in this area didn't go to the next level until Larry and I founded EQUIP. We did it specifically to partner with other organizations. In the beginning, we approached two hundred non-profit organizations and offered to train their leaders. We had high hopes, but only two American groups responded positively. So we started with them and did our best to add value to them and train leaders.

Eventually we started partnering with organizations outside of the United States. Our strategy was simple. We offered to add value to organizations that were already doing work of significance by training leaders. As the leaders grew and became more effective in making a difference, the organizations became more effective. If you want to grow any organization, focus on growing the leaders.

Now, two decades later, we have partners in every nation in the world. And we have trained five million leaders. It is a beautiful picture of finding like-minded and like-valued people and the amazing compounding effect that it has when you live intentionally.

## Remember, Everyone Starts Small

One of my worries about telling you my story is that it might sound bigger and better than it really is. Don't forget that I started out in Hillham, and I spent twenty-six years working to add value to people before Larry and I started EQUIP. Is it true that EQUIP has trained more than five million people? Yes. Do Larry and I deserve the credit for that? No. It is truly the result of too many partnerships to name—with the original board of directors who bankrolled the entire organization, with the subsequent board members who supported the vision mentally, emotionally, spiritually, and financially, with Doug Carter, who raised funds for EQUIP for twenty years, with literally *hundreds* of organizations who partnered with us, with translators, with volunteers.

Every person who has partnered with me over the years on this significance journey—whether at a church, with EQUIP, or at one of my companies—deserves credit, just as everyone who partners with you will deserve it. As you look for like-valued people to partner with, make sure they possess what I call "the great separators." All of my most effective partners shared these qualities that make a difference. They possessed commitment. I always asked for that up front, because commitment separates the players from the pretenders. They thought beyond themselves, because to make a difference, people have to put others first. They had the capacity to dream big dreams. I wanted to partner with people who thought without limitations. And they possessed passion. This was most important, because passion is contagious and influences others. It invites energy and it creates movement.

Perhaps at the time I could not have told you that these were the exact things I was looking for, because I didn't have enough experience yet to articulate them. But I followed my intuition. I sensed that much more energy was required to do something significant. And I knew I'd need a group of like-valued people around me—people who wanted to make a difference.

I cannot overstate the importance of learning the lesson of teaming up with other people who want to make a difference. This is the multiplying factor that makes it possible for an individual to change a family, a community, a city, a country—the world. If you have a vision of significance that promises to help other people, and you partner with others who share that same vision, there is no limit to what can be done. The only other factor you need to come into play is timing, which I discuss in the final two chapters of this book.

Author and speaker Brian Tracy wrote, "You are a living magnet. You are invariably attracting to your life people and situations in harmony with your dominant thoughts." Or to put it the way my mother did when I was a kid, "Birds of a feather flock together." It may sound corny, but it's true.

In *The 21 Irrefutable Laws of Leadership*, I wrote about the Law of Magnetism, which says that who you are is who you attract. This principle shows up in everything you do, all that you say, how you present yourself, and where you go. If you are passionate about significance, you will tend to attract people who want to be significant. Your energy and enthusiasm will be so contagious that people will want to be around you. People will want what you have. You will find people drawn to you asking for a taste from your significance cup. And once they sip from that vessel, believe me, they'll want more.

## With Like-Valued Partners, Impact Can Grow

When you partner with like-valued people, there's no telling what kind of positive result might come out of it. I recently became aware of a great example of this when I was the keynote speaker at the national convention for Defender, a service company based in Indiana. Dave Lindsey, the company's CEO, said that when he started the company, he had a desire to have a company that was generous in giving to others.

"One of the reasons I think we give as corporations is because we know it's important to work at a giving company," says Lindsey.

But Lindsey says that many organizations get it wrong because they don't think in terms of true partnership. They ask employees to adopt their values instead of finding places where their values line up.

Lindsey explains: "We say, 'OK, the company's going to give here, so be excited,' instead of going to the employee and saying, 'What are you excited about?

Where's your heart? What nonprofit is important to you? And we'll give there.' We kind of flipped the script.... We're now fueling their passion instead of trying to create passion where it didn't exist."

How did Lindsey do that? He asked employees to declare what mattered to them first, to choose where they wanted to serve and give. Then Defender would support them. The result? Participation skyrocketed.

Lindsey calls this effort the Super Service Challenge. Here's how it works: He gives his employees time off to serve nonprofit organizations. The only stipulation is that the organizations being served have to be recognized nonprofits, 501(c)(3)s, for the employees to get time off at Defender's expense. Defender also helps these volunteers to raise money to give to the nonprofits they serve.

The process Defender came up with was simple. They suggested:

1. **Grab Your Co-workers.** We suggest three or more people.
2. **Pick a Nonprofit.** Choose any registered 501(c)(3) nonprofit.
3. **Go Serve.** Serve the nonprofit as a team.
4. **Share Your Story.** Create a video sharing your experience. Your video can win money for the nonprofit you served![25]

What started at Defender grew. In 2011, eighty teams in Indianapolis participated and together they gave away $200,000 to their causes. Soon others began to take notice, including NFL quarterback Drew Brees. The next year Brees became a partner and took the Challenge to New Orleans. More than 250 teams participated and gave away more than $1 million.

In 2013, it spread to forty-two states, where over seven hundred companies fielded more than 250 teams serving people and giving away $1.6 million.[26]

Although the challenge started within Dave Lindsey's company as part of his workplace culture, it is spreading quickly. And it's still growing. His next goal is to make the Super Service Challenge an international effort.

In our busy and hectic lives, it is sometimes easy for us to overlook or forget the power of partnership. However, when you live with intentional significance, your inclusion of others also has to become intentional. As you make plans, you must involve other people and invite them to become partners. To receive their full engagement, you must be ready to commit, compromise, sacrifice, and connect with them. You don't get more than you give. But when you give those things, they are likely to reciprocate. And there's an amazing and powerful compounding effect that takes place.

# Intentional Application:
# Partner with Like-Valued People

## What Are Your Values?

To find like-valued people, it helps to know what you're looking for. Take some time to think about the values most important to you for making a difference in the lives of others. As a starting point, look at the twelve things I look for:

Thinks of Others First
Thinks Bigger than Self
Passion That's Contagious
Complementary Gifts
Great at Support
Can-Do Spirit
Expanded Influence
Activist Mindset
Ladder Builder
Stands Out from the Crowd
Synergy Creator
Difference Maker

Which of those is important to you? Check them.

What additional qualities or characteristics not listed are important to you? Write them down. This becomes your starting list for finding like-valued people.

## Who Shares Your Values?

Because I travel a lot, I'm often met at airports by drivers who don't know me. Some of them create a sign with my name and hold it up. It's up to me to find them. Others have a completely different approach. They get a photo me, often from one of my books, so they know what I look like, and they take responsibility for finding me.

If you completed the previous Intentional Application exercise, you now know what like-valued people look like. Take responsibility for finding them! Who in your life desires significance and shares your values? When you find them, connect with them. Start building your relationships with them so that you're ready to take the next step . . .

## Find a Place to Partner with Them *Today*

Once you've made a relational connection with someone, it's time to find your significance connection. Either you have a dream that you can share with the hope that he or she will join you, or that person has a dream you need to listen to with the hope that you can join in.

Who initiates with the dream is not important. Some people discover the dream and then the team. Others join the team to discover the dream. What matters is that you partner with other like-minded and like-valued people to make a difference for others. That's how you achieve a life that matters.

# AT A TIME THAT MAKES A DIFFERENCE

# 9

## Live with a Sense of Anticipation

We're entering the home stretch in our discussion of intentional living, and I now want to focus on helping you to make a difference at a time that makes a difference. When is that time? Well, it's *now* of course. But simply saying "take action now" doesn't equip you to make the most of every day, does it? So what I want to do is help you to develop the right kind of mindset for performing acts of significance, and the first thing I need to do is guide you to live with a sense of anticipation. To help you understand that, I'll tell you the next part of my story.

### Something I Didn't Anticipate

When I resigned from Skyline to focus on making a difference in the lives of more people through EQUIP and my companies, I had a great sense of anticipation. At that time I was approaching fifty years old, I was working every day in my sweet spot, I was adding value to people, and I was beginning to experience the compounding effect of nearly three decades of intentional living.

But I was also starting to feel a little frustrated by the amount of time it took for me and members of my team to travel from San Diego to various cities around the country for conferences, consulting, and speaking dates. So I asked my assistant Linda Eggers to do a time-cost analysis of my travel for the previous twelve months. What she discovered blew me away. In one year, I had spent the equivalent of twenty-eight days flying to hub cities, just to make travel connections from San Diego. *Twenty-eight days!* Can you imagine losing an entire month of your life that way?

As I've already told you, I'm highly strategic about how I spend my time. I had spent five decades figuring out how to make the most of my days. And now I was finding out that I was spending 8 percent of my year on planes just going from point A to point B. And that meant the consultants who worked for my companies were spending a similar percentage of time taking extra flights, because the majority of our clients were east of the Mississippi River.

I loved everything about San Diego. I loved the topography. I loved being near the ocean. I loved the perfect climate. It's a beautiful place. But that was the day I knew we needed to move the company. If I wanted to compound my significance and make the most of every day, we had to move ourselves and the companies away from the West Coast. To anticipate doing significant acts, you must *position* yourself to immediately take action. You can't take action if you're spending too much of your time trying to get to the front lines. You need to *be* on the front lines.

> You can't take action if you're spending too much of your time trying to get to the front lines. You need to *be* on the front lines.

Where would we go? I loved New York, but it wasn't central enough. Besides, it's an expensive place to live, and I had to take into account the cost of living for all the people who worked with us. The only three cities I seriously considered were centrally located airline hubs: Chicago, Dallas, and Atlanta. When I examined the benefits of flying out of these three cities to reach our most common work destinations, the cities were all even. So the next thing I looked at was the cost of living. That eliminated Chicago. Besides, I grew up in a place where I had to shovel snow every winter, and I had no great desire to go back to that. I like it warm! That meant I was choosing between Dallas and Atlanta.

We ultimately chose Atlanta because we thought it positioned us best for making a difference. The cost of living was affordable for everyone. The climate was good. And the location was fantastic. About 80 percent of America's population is within a two-hour flight of the Atlanta airport.

## Who Will Make the Significance Trip?

Once the location decision was made, the next consideration was the team itself. I sat down and created a list of all the people in the company. There were sixty-five people working in my three organizations who we felt were essential team players. We had worked hard to build these teams of like-minded and like-valued people. The question was who would choose to make the move. Half of the families were California natives, and they loved where they lived. That region was all they knew, so moving across the country would be a drastic change for them. What would they do? I estimated that about half the people on that list would make the move.

When I gathered the team to tell everyone we were going to move the companies' headquarters to Atlanta, I knew the news would come as a shock. I laid the whole thing out for them—the missed opportunities because we were in California. The anticipation I felt for greater significance if we moved to a central airline hub. The homework we'd done to make sure the quality of life there would be good for everyone. I have to admit, it was very emotional.

When I finished speaking, the people didn't have to speak a word. I could feel that they were with me. I didn't ask anyone to raise their hands or give a sign of support. In fact, when I was done speaking, I actually got up and left the room before there could be any real discussion, because I wanted to give everyone time to process it. I didn't want to sell them. I wanted them to make the choice best for them.

One team member actually followed me out and said, "You can count me in."

What amazed me was that everyone felt that way.

Ultimately, only two people chose to stay in San Diego—and they remained for family reasons. Not only did the sixty-three other people make the move to Atlanta, but five years later only one family had moved back to California.

All these people were committed to the significance

mission we were now clearly walking. My personal vision had become a collective vision; my dream, their dream. They wanted to add value to people as much as I did. No, it went beyond the desire to make a difference. They went with me because they *anticipated* making a difference!

## Intentional Anticipation

I've noted that many people want to make a difference when they are confronted with a crisis or tragedy. They will pick up their phones and donate money to Haiti or Japan after a horrific and devastating earthquake. They will donate clothes or supplies for tsunami relief. They will volunteer their time after an unexpected crisis in our country, such as a destructive hurricane or a child abduction.

When urgent things happen, we Americans generally have the heart to respond in that moment, as we did after 9/11. This type of call to perform significant acts occurs every once in a while. While rising to this call is good, and I would certainly encourage you to serve in these kinds of situations, I want to talk about a different kind of urgency in this chapter. It is not a momentary sense of urgency that comes during a crisis. No, this is a kind of urgency that is proactive. It's based on anticipation.

To me, *anticipation* is a wonderfully proactive and intentional word for *seeking out* significance. People with anticipation *plan* to be significant. They *expect* to live a life that matters every day. They *prepare* to do significant acts. They *position* themselves physically, mentally, emotion-

> ***Anticipation* is a wonderfully proactive and intentional word for *seeking out* significance.**

ally, and financially to make a difference in the lives of others. Their sense of anticipation for significance draws them forward.

What does a strong sense of anticipation do for us? It does five things:

## 1. Anticipation Causes Us to Value Today

Every day I anticipate that I will find an opportunity to do a significant act by adding value to someone. I look at my daily calendar and think about the potential times and places that I can do this. Anticipation causes my mind to look for new significant moments and, when possible, to create them. This has become a discipline of mine. And it can become one of yours.

When you live with intentionality, you *know* and *understand* that every day is your time to make a difference. It's not someday, one day, or maybe tomorrow. It's *today*. You will have the time to make a difference if you want to, so it's about living with the understanding that you can and then taking action.

> When you live with intentionality, you *know* and *understand* that every day is your time to make a difference.

This sense of anticipation was already strong in me when I moved to Atlanta, but it went to another level a year later after my experience at our company Christmas party. I had been dancing that night when suddenly I didn't feel very well. One of my team members who was saying good night hugged me, and when she felt the back of my neck, she pointed out that I was in a cold sweat.

I quickly went from feeling bad to worse. Suddenly there was a horrible pain in my chest. I knew I was having a heart attack, so I lay down on the floor as they called for an ambulance.

While I waited, I told everyone how much I loved and appreciated them. I wanted them to know how important they were to me and how valued they were.

When the ambulance arrived, they took me to Grady Hospital in downtown Atlanta. If you're injured with a gunshot or knife wound, Grady is where you want to be. But not if you're having a heart attack. They didn't have the facility or staff to do the tests I needed for my heart problem. Things did not look good for me.

That was when my assistant, Linda, remembered that six months earlier I had given her the card of a top cardiologist in Nashville. I had met the man when I had lunch with Sam Moore, who was my book publisher at the time. Dr. John Bright Cage had handed me his card and said, "As a doctor, I want to talk to you. You're in trouble. You're overweight and a candidate for a heart attack."

I pretty much dismissed him. I didn't like his message. I told him I handled stress really well and there was nothing to worry about.

"God called me to take care of you," he said. "Take my card, John. Don't lose it, because you are going to need it. And when you do, call me."

I could tell this doctor's intentions were good, so I accepted his card. I didn't give what he said much credence, nor did I value the card. Why would I? I'd recently had a physical and had been told my heart was healthy. Besides, he lived in Nashville—five hours from my home near Atlanta. The likelihood of our paths ever crossing again was relatively small. Despite all this, I gave the card to Linda, and I never gave it another thought.

But Linda sure did. She is the kind of woman who is always prepared. Back then, before smartphones, she usually carried her Rolodex in the backseat of her car. Thank God she did that night. Her quick thinking and preparation likely saved my life.

Linda called Dr. Cage at 2:00 a.m. to tell him the situation. He knew exactly what needed to be done. It was as if he somehow had been expecting the call. Dr. Cage quickly made arrangements to transfer me to Emory Hospital. Somehow within fifteen minutes, he found a cardiologist to ride in the ambulance with me, without whom I might not have made it. When we arrived at Emory, Dr. Jeff Marshall, the head of cardiology there, and his brilliant team were waiting for me.

"I don't know who you are," said Dr. Marshall greeting the ambulance, "but all four of us were awakened by Dr. Cage to meet you here."

They immediately rolled me into the emergency room.

For a few very long and scary hours, my condition was unstable. When I entered the first hospital I had three nurses and one doctor watching over me. At Emory a couple of hours later, there were suddenly four of the best doctors in the country overseeing my situation. Although I wasn't clear on everything that was happening, one thing I was certain of—*more* doctors in the room was not a good sign.

During this time I was physically very uncomfortable. But *spiritually* I was at peace. Before that incident, I had often wondered how I would feel when I faced death's door. Now I no longer have to wonder. I was not afraid. You don't really know if you're going to be afraid of death until you've been close

> You don't really know if you're going to be afraid of death until you've been close enough to touch it, taste it, and smell it.

enough to touch it, taste it, and smell it. For two and a half hours, I was a hairbreadth from death's door, and yet I was as relaxed and calm as could be.

The only thing I asked of Dr. Marshall that day was to tell me if I was dying.

"You're not dying yet, but if we can't turn this around, you will," he said.

"Just tell me," I said, fading in and out of consciousness.

Although I had no fear and no regrets, there was one question I kept asking God and myself that fateful night: "Is my purpose complete?" You see, I was only fifty-one. I felt that a person like me couldn't be done! I was too young to have fulfilled my full purpose—my complete *why*. However, as I lay in the hospital bed that night, I knew without a doubt that I had done my best and absolutely could look back upon my life with no regrets about the significance path I had taken. That realization gave me a great deal of peace and comfort.

I will confess to you, I was somewhat surprised I had such peace about my life. The feeling of calm and lack of regret took me aback. If you had given me a phone so that I could take care of any unfinished business, I'm not sure who I would have called. Though I didn't know I was going to have that heart attack, what I found out was that it would become the most amazing spiritual experience of my life. It gave me the greatest confidence in my faith. It proved my faith to me, and I don't question it—ever.

The doctors did pull me through, obviously. Dr. Marshall told me that if I'd had the same heart attack a year earlier, I would have died because the procedure and equipment they used to save me hadn't been available the year before.

After a full recovery, I felt a heightened responsibility to steward my gifts and opportunities. My sense of anticipation was sharpened. I believed strongly that since I was still alive, I probably hadn't totally fulfilled my purpose. There was still more work to do. My purpose is the reason I lived.

Coming out of that experience, here's what I don't know and what I do know.

I don't know when I will die.

I do know that discovering and fulfilling my purpose has allowed me to live my life without regrets.

What about you? If you came to death's door today, would you be facing it without regrets? Do you know why you're here, and have you done your best to fulfill your purpose? If not, you need to find your *why*—the sooner the better. The moment you start to understand what it is, that's the moment you can start living it with a strong sense of anticipation.

My life was forever changed when I had my heart attack, not just because of the physical ramifications or the change in lifestyle I had to make. And not just because of the faith and peace I experienced in the moment I was facing the possibility of my death. What changed? Up until then, I had assumed my days instead of numbering them. The difference between assuming and numbering your days is huge.

> The difference between assuming and numbering your days is huge.

Here's what I mean. Until that experience, I always thought I had more time. That day I realized I might not have any more time. I faced the prospect that it might actually be game-over. That realization created a sense of urgency and *anticipation* I had never before felt. It clarified how much I really wanted to make my life count. It was as if God spoke to me and said, "I am not done with you yet. Make the most of the time you have left!"

Nothing lights your fire faster than being given another shot at life. When I survived the heart attack, there was no doubt that I was on a mission. There was a plan much bigger than my own to fulfill and accomplish. I've never looked at life the same since.

I hope you don't have to experience a heart attack to develop the strong sense of anticipation that helps you value today. Whether you know it or not, your days are numbered, just as mine are. But more important, on any given day, when you have a chance to add value to others and perform an act of significance, you may never get that chance again. The moment can pass, and most of the time you don't get that moment back. The opportunity is gone, and the person who could have been helped has gone on his way. That's why you need to seize it.

## 2. Anticipation Prompts Us to Prepare

Wayne Gretzky is undoubtedly the greatest hockey player ever. I remember hearing him explain in an interview why he was so much more successful than the other hockey players in the game. "Most hockey players follow the puck on the ice," he said. "I never skate to where the puck is. I skate to where it is going." That is a great illustration of anticipation.

> "Most hockey players follow the puck on the ice. I never skate to where the puck is. I skate to where it is going."
> —Wayne Gretzky

Having a strong sense of anticipation changes the way you look at everything, and it makes you prepare differently. For example, every year I search to find the one word that will help me to focus my efforts and attention for the coming year. (I look for just one word because I can't handle a whole sentence!) During that year, I use that word to find many significant lessons and experiences. Identifying this word and using it as a guide has become a discipline for me.

One year the word was *failure*. I decided that every time I was confronted with failure, I would make sure I understood that it wasn't final by learning from it. It helped me embrace the idea that failed plans should not be interpreted as a failed vision. Plans rarely stay the same, and are scrapped or adjusted as needed. Vision is only refined by failure. It's important to remain stubborn about your vision, but flexible with your plan.

Another year the word was *miracles*, because I felt

that almost every problem, obstacle, or failure had a miracle opportunity in it—a possibility that I didn't see. That year I continually asked myself, "Is this miracle material? Can this be lifted up? Is this an opportunity to help others?"

Another year I chose the word *success*. Every day I thought, *What is success? Who is successful? Why are they successful? How can I help others be successful?*

In 2013 and 2014 for the first time the same word impressed itself upon me: *transformation*. That word stirred the mission of EQUIP and was the catalyst for this book. I initially wanted to write a book on transformational leadership, but I knew that before I could see a big vision of transformation, I had to plant the seeds of significance. I believe that if you do many intentional acts of significance, you can become a transformational leader.

When you anticipate that you *can* and *will* make a difference, you prepare differently—for your day, for your year, for your work, for your family, in how you see problems, and in how you see opportunities. Anticipation changes everything.

> When you anticipate that you *can* and *will* make a difference, you prepare differently.

## 3. Anticipation Helps Us Generate Good Ideas

When we possess an attitude of anticipation, we expect to come up with good ideas to help us make a difference. Whenever I meet with my team, whether it's to solve a problem, develop a new product or service for one of the companies, or create an initiative to add value to people, we never go into the meeting believing we *won't* come up with good ideas. We expect to succeed. We anticipate positive solutions, and that helps us to come up with them.

I heard about an amazing example of how anticipation feeds innovation when I learned about a teenager named Easton LaChappelle. When he was fourteen, he decided he wanted to build a robotic hand. He started surfing the Internet to learn about electronics. Then he pulled together his Legos, some small motors, electrical tubing, fishing line, and tape. And he built a robotic hand with articulating fingers that he could control remotely. That's a pretty good story of anticipated success. But that's not where his story ends.

When LaChappelle was at the state science fair in his home state of Colorado, he met a seven-year-old girl who had a prosthetic limb. Her professionally manufactured hand could do less than the robotic hand he had designed—hers could only open and close—yet it had cost her family $80,000. That's when the lightbulb turned on. He knew his *why*. He would figure out how to make high-functioning prosthetics that were affordable.

He got to work in his bedroom at home, and by the time he was sixteen, he had built a prototype prosthesis using 3-D printing technology. It had cost under $400 to make. LaChappelle later went on to build a prosthetic arm with articulating fingers that could be controlled by an electroencephalogram (EEG) headband that measures brain waves. He produced it for under $500![27] Then he announced that the technology he had developed would be open-source, meaning he was giving it away so that anyone in the world would be free to use it and improve upon it without having to pay him for it.[28] When you have an idea, if you think it's the only one you'll ever come up with, you hoard it. However, if you anticipate that you will have more ideas, you're willing to share it.

> When you have an idea, if you think it's the only one you'll ever come up with, you hoard it. However, if you anticipate that you will have more ideas, you're willing to share it.

What's LaChappelle doing now? He has graduated from high school. He started a company to build prosthetic limbs at low cost, and he's working with

NASA, helping them with robotics. He continues to come up with ideas and help people, because he anticipates that he will.

How is your attitude when it comes to solutions to help other people? Do you anticipate success? Do you believe you will come up with ideas? Do you have enough confidence in your ability to add value that you're willing to share your ideas and solutions? Develop anticipation, and you will start to have more confidence in your ability to make a difference.

## 4. Anticipation Prompts Us to Look for Ways to Help Others

When I left Skyline, one of the things I knew I wanted to do was add value to ten people with great potential. So I started thinking about who should be on the list. There were only two criteria. First, I had to be able to add value to them in an area where I knew I could make a substantial impact. Second, they needed to have some success under their belt or be on the cusp of success, and be in need of my help to make a breakthrough. That would ensure that whatever value I added to them would compound. That would make my time and effort like investing in a blue-chip stock where I knew I would get my best return on investment.

In many ways, the ten people I chose were better, faster, and smarter than I was, which was why I wanted to saddle up alongside them, find out what they needed, and give it to them—no questions asked and no conditions.

I very diligently and methodically went after those ten, but I never told them my purpose—unless they asked. In the cases when someone did ask, I'd simply respond by saying, "I want to serve you." But my true desire was to quietly add value to their lives without revealing my reasons.

Doing this sharpened my sense of anticipation, and as I helped them, my belief that I could add value to people only got stronger. The success of others was soon more important to me than my own success. I knew I had experiences and knowledge I could offer to help people. I began to get a bigger thrill watching and celebrating someone else's win than celebrating my own.

It's been twenty years since I created that first list of people I wanted to pour into, and today I still keep a list of the names of ten people I desire to serve. Over the years, the names on the list have changed, though there are a few from that original list that remain. I've served some people for a season and some for a reason. A few I keep serving and plan to serve for a lifetime. I always want to add value to each person on the list. Of course, over time, my goal has grown beyond serving just ten people. But that original list was a catalyst to help me remain intentional in adding value to others, and maintaining that sense of anticipation.

## 5. Anticipation Helps Us Possess an Abundance Mindset

The previous advantage of anticipation leads to this next one—having an abundance mindset. People live in one of two different kinds of worlds. One world comes from having a scarcity mindset. You cannot give what you do not have. Scarcity thinking has nothing to give. It is preoccupied with receiving. Scarcity thinking is all about me. It says, "There's not enough to go around. I had better get something for myself and hold on to it with all I have." People who live in the world of scarcity think, *There's only one pie, so I'd better get as big a slice as I can before it's all gone.*

People who live in the world of abundance think very differently. They know there's always more. As others scramble and try to grab their slice of pie, people with an abundance mindset think, *That's OK. We'll just bake another pie.*

> **People with an abundance mindset think, *That's OK. We'll just bake another pie.***

Abundance thinking is the mindset of people of significance, and it has nothing to do with how much they have. They may not have financial wealth. They may not live in great situations. But whatever they have, they are willing to share because they don't worry about running out. They can be their brothers' keepers, because they believe there is more to be found, more to be created. If there isn't a way now, another one will be invented.

What may surprise you is that two people who occupy the same space, face the exact same circumstances, and receive the same opportunities can live in these two different worlds. One person can be restricted by thinking in terms of scarcity. The other can have an abundance mindset that makes nearly anything possible. Their thinking, more than almost anything else, has an impact on whether they live as haves or have-nots.

When I talk to people about abundance and scarcity mindsets, I sometimes ask, "Which would you *prefer* to have?" Everybody raises their hand for abundance, yet many struggle because they are mentally stuck in the scarcity world.

So I'll ask you the question: Which world would you prefer to live in, scarcity or abundance? If having an abundance mindset is difficult for you, the good news is that you can change. You can use *anticipa-*

*tion* to help you change the
way you think and act. How?
By practicing positive anticipation for yourself and others. Anticipation is a key that

> Anticipation is a
> key that unlocks the
> doors to abundance
> thinking.

unlocks the doors to abundance thinking.

"Doors?" you may be asking. "Don't you mean
*door*?"

No. Expecting there to be only one door is scarcity
thinking.

Let me explain how anticipation begins and grows
in your life.

There is a door of opportunity before you. Maybe
you see it; maybe you don't. But it is there. If you have
positive anticipation, you assume it's there, and you
make the effort to find it, and if you are diligent in that
effort, you will find it. But know this. It may be locked,
and it may require a lot of effort for you to unlock it
and walk through it. Are you willing to give it a try?
*Do you believe you can?* Some people will try and some
people won't. I hope you're someone who's willing.

What usually makes the difference? Anticipation.
When you have positive anticipation, you believe that
you can open the door. And if you anticipate that
something positive could be on the other side, you
will try to open it.

So let's say you are willing. You do have positive

anticipation, which, by the way, is a choice, because we don't know what will be behind that door. If you walk through that door, do you know what you will find? More doors. There is not one door of opportu-

> **There is not one door of opportunity. There is not one door to significance. There is a series of doors.**

nity. There is not one door to significance. There is a series of doors. What keeps you moving forward, unlocking those doors? Anticipation!

Finding and going through one door is an event. Going through many doors is a lifestyle. That requires an abundance mindset. Every time you open another door, your anticipation gets stronger and is validated. Over time, it can become part of your DNA. And if you keep going through doors, you will create success, and you will have a chance to achieve significance. You will make a difference. It's almost inevitable.

Sadly, too many people have a scarcity mindset and lack positive anticipation. As a result, they never open the first door. Unopened doors reinforce scarcity thinking and scarcity living. Others do open that first door, but when it doesn't offer what they expected, they become disappointed and abandon the pursuit. They give up.

Don't let that happen to you. Don't let the gap between expectation and reality disappoint you. Don't let it kill your sense of anticipation. Keep searching for doors and opening them. And remember that with each open door, your anticipation will increase and so will abundance.

If you find this difficult, then begin changing your thinking by recalling your past successes and keeping them in the forefront of your mind. Think about risks you took that led to rewards. Think about opportunities you pursued that gave you success. Think about the lessons you learned even when things didn't go your way, and how you later benefitted from those lessons. Rely on these memories. They can give you a frame of reference to anticipate good things happening in your future. If you anticipate the positives and couple that with a desire to help and add value to others, you can make a difference.

## Building a House of Significance

The journey of positive anticipation that I just shared with you has been a reality in my life. To me, living a life that matters is like building a house. The process started as I opened the first door, which was *I want to make a difference*. Once I went through that first doorway, I entered my first room of significance. And I discovered some wonderful ways that I could make a difference in the lives of others.

Each day that I lived in that room I intentionally tried to add value to someone. Some days were better than others, but each day was an intentional effort to help someone. I experienced more wins than losses, and each time I added value to someone, it added value to me. My intentional sowing resulted in eventual reaping. Out of my sense of abundance, I looked for more significance. Anticipation fed my desire to do more.

With each day, making a difference unlocked another door. When the second door opened it allowed me to live in two rooms. The first room, *I want to make a difference*, was now joined with the second room, *doing something that makes a difference*. That room allowed me to discover my strengths, the things I could do better than anything else. Those strengths included leading, communicating, and connecting. As I practiced those strengths, my significance became more focused and that laser concentration began bringing a higher return. It was in this room that I found my purpose, my *why*. Knowing my reason for existence empowered me to become more strategic about everything, but above all else in the area of significance. What more could I do to make a difference?

My anticipation fed my questioning until I found an answer that caused me to search for the third door in my significance journey. With anticipation, I unlocked the third door, which is doing something that makes a difference *with people who make a difference*. This new room was filled with people who were potential partners in significance. I'm grateful for this because of my personal limitations. Alone I can only do so much. The compounding potential and return of working with others makes my sense of anticipation soar.

> The compounding potential and return of working with others makes my sense of anticipation soar.

During the first few years I was in this room, I constantly looked for people who could add value to me. This limited me and the significance I could achieve. But then I realized that I should be focusing on adding value to the people who partnered with me. Today, as I live in this area, I have one desire: to find people who are like-minded and like-valued so that I can lift them and their levels of significance.

For many years, my house of significance had only three rooms. It seemed to me that my dream house was finished. Yet, the longer I connected with others and worked with them and served them, it became increasingly clear that they had a desire to transform individuals, communities, and even countries. Soon I was asking questions about transformational leaders and what qualities they possess.

I watched them and followed them and found

another door of opportunity. This final room was *at a time that makes a difference*. People who open this door live with intentionality. They live with anticipation and seize opportunities to make a difference. They live with an urgency that empowers them to make each day a masterpiece of significance. Their intensity and focus cannot be denied. They anticipate the needs of others. Their behavior backs up their beliefs, and their actions underscore and build more anticipation. They are living the significance cycle: anticipation, action, abundance, anticipation, action, abundance. When I understood this and partnered with others, we were able to make a difference together at a whole new level.

If you possess an abundance mindset, this probably makes sense to you. Fantastic! Don't hesitate. Move forward.

If you have a scarcity mindset, it may be harder for you to live with positive anticipation. If you want to change, consider this. If you live with a scarcity mindset, you will get what you expect. You will have scarcity. Guaranteed. No one experiences abundance while anticipating scarcity. So why not try abundance? At best, you'll experience abundance. At worst, you'll get the scar-

> No one experiences abundance while anticipating scarcity. So why not try on abundance?

city you've already been experiencing. You have nothing to lose. Believe, anticipate, take action, give, and see what happens. It could change your life.

## Anticipating Transformation

One of the places where my strong sense of anticipation has played out, and where people could easily see it, is in my nonprofit organization, EQUIP. In 2003, several years after my brother Larry and I started EQUIP, I got a strong sense that we should try to train one million leaders in countries around the world. We launched what we called a million-leader mandate.

There were people who thought we were crazy, that we were striving to do something that was impossible. But that didn't discourage us. Our sense of anticipation was strong. We partnered with people and organizations first in India, Indonesia, and the Philippines. Then in other parts of Asia. Then in Africa and Europe. Then in South and Central America. In 2008, we hit the goal. And then we trained another million leaders, and another. As of 2013, we had trained more than five million leaders worldwide. Our sense of anticipation had paid off.

But in 2013, something else happened. I realized that I had made a mistake. I had assumed that training leaders would automatically make a positive difference in the lives of others in the countries where we had done the training. But I have discovered that giving leaders training does not make them transformational in the lives of others. They don't automatically want to make a difference. They don't live out intentional significance.

As a result of this realization, our leadership team began asking, "What did we miss?" After much soul-searching and many long hours of discussions, here was our conclusion: The training we had done was educational, not transformational.

Training leaders was our objective, so we had focused on the lessons we taught more than the lives we hoped to change. We kept statistics on training but generated relatively few stories of significance. We weren't making the difference we had hoped for. What would I do?

This was a real quandary for me. As the founder and leader of the organization, I had to make a decision. My heart was encouraging me to be strong and declare that we needed to make a bold change. But my pride in my reputation made me want to stay the course. It said, "EQUIP is recognized as a world-class training organization. Accept the applause. Receive the respect given by people around the world. At your age, enjoy the end of a wonderful journey."

For weeks, my heart and my desire to preserve my reputation battled against one another.

Finally the EQUIP board came together to discuss the organization's future. We talked very frankly, and they shared words of wisdom. The support and love I felt from them were overwhelming. These board members had walked this journey with me, and now they were willing to let me decide our direction. They would let me choose whether to strike forward in a new direction, or be satisfied with our past accomplishments.

In those moments, my pride made one last push for me to settle for what I had. That was the easy road. "Let someone younger and more capable take the difficult road of striving for significance," it said to me. "You've paid your dues, and now is the time to walk away to a less demanding life."

But my heart wouldn't let my pride win. My desire for significance—and my overwhelming sense of anticipation that we *could* make a difference—was stronger, and it won out. We would change direction. We would start again, striving for significance.

Once again I felt the adrenaline surge through my body. I recognized that feeling. I had felt that same surge of energy in 1965 when I was challenged with that same question: What do you dream about? My dream had not retired. My journey of significance was not over. This was the time to make a difference. To fulfill my calling of adding value to people, I needed to lead EQUIP to another level. I needed to lead the charge as we helped trained leaders to become transformational leaders.

A transformational leader intentionally engages people to think and act in such a way that it makes a positive difference in their lives and in the lives of others. Now more than ever, I wanted to pursue that dream. I followed my heart that day, and I shared with the board that EQUIP would become a catalyst for one million stories of transformation. I also committed to writing this book.

> A transformational leader intentionally engages people to think and act in such a way that it makes a positive difference in their lives and in the lives of others.

Undoubtedly, this is also your time to make a difference. If you live with positive anticipation, you can do it. Maybe you are already doing it. Or maybe you're in the preparation stages—searching for the first door of opportunity, or for the second or third doors. Where you are in the process doesn't matter. As long as you are engaged in it and anticipate positive results, you're on your way.

> Where you are in the process doesn't matter. As long as you are engaged in it and anticipate positive results, you're on your way.

The only thing left for you to do is understand how to seize opportunities to make a difference. And that is the subject of the final chapter of this book.

## Intentional Application:
## Live with a Sense of Anticipation

### Anticipating Today's Impact

When you woke up this morning, what was your mindset related to making a difference? Did you *believe* you could make a difference? Did you *expect* to make a difference? Or did you even think about it at all?

What can you do to ratchet up your sense of anticipation every day? How can you remind yourself to make this a part of your everyday existence? What can you do to remind yourself that *now* is the time to find ways to help and add value to people? Perhaps you need to put a Post-it note on your bathroom mirror or computer screen. Maybe you need to pin up a photograph of someone you helped in the past so that you see it every day and are inspired to take action. Maybe you need to make a message of anticipation your home screen on your phone or computer desktop. Maybe you need a daily reminder sent to you on your phone at an opportune time. Or maybe you can ask someone to hold you accountable for taking action every day or week.

Do whatever is necessary to help you develop a sense of positive anticipation for making a difference. Don't settle, as I was tempted to do when wrestling with the issue of EQUIP.

## Get Ready

In what ways are you preparing to make a difference? My old mentor John Wooden used to say, "When opportunity comes, it's too late to prepare." Are you preparing? Are you anticipating your chance to make a difference? When you get that chance, will you be ready?

I suggest that you do two things to help you be ready. First, gather your resources. Think about what you have that you can use to help others. Second, create margins in your life. Many people fail to make a difference because they are so busy. They move so fast that they don't see the opportunities, or they have so much to do that they believe they don't have the time to stop and help. Don't be one of those people!

## Do You Believe in Abundance?

Which are you: a scarcity person or an abundance person? If you're not an abundance person, follow the advice in the chapter. Look to your past for inspiration. Make a list of your past successes. Add to that list every advantage, gift, or benefit you've ever received that you did not earn. Add to the list the positive lessons you've learned from your mistakes and failures.

If you give this exercise the time it deserves, you'll come up with a very long list. In fact, if you keep the list handy during the next several days, weeks, or month, you might be able to surprise yourself with how many positive things you come up with.

Now here's the point. Look at the list. If scarcity is the norm, how in the world have you experienced so many positive things? Abundance is out there. You just need to believe in it and anticipate that you will benefit from it. Make the mental shift to abundance. And whenever you are tempted to feel discouraged or cynical, pull out that long list and review it again.

# 10

## Be Urgent about Seizing Significance Opportunities

In November of 1989, I was standing in the kitchen of our home in San Diego when I heard on the news that the Berlin Wall was being torn down. It was clear to me that without a doubt, history was being made that very moment. I was headed to my home office, but I turned to Margaret and said, "We need to go there. I think we should get the kids on a plane and go now. They've got to see this."

Then I went to my office, as I usually did each morning, because there were a couple of things on my schedule that needed my attention.

I got absorbed in my work and within minutes, the urgency of trying to get to Berlin faded. I thought, *Berlin can wait.* And the moment slipped away.

Forever.

I have always felt frustration over that decision. Going to Berlin with my kids to see the wall come down was a once-in-a-lifetime opportunity. I wanted to show them what can happen to a country when leadership goes bad. Because of the division of Berlin after World War II, families got separated. Then the East Germans made their own people prisoners by putting up a wall. That wall was a symbol of evil and corrupt leadership. And its destruction was a symbol of hope and positive leadership, not by a government but by the people.

I wanted my children to see that it was ordinary people who were taking down the wall. They had come to a place where they said, "No more." I wanted my kids to experience the celebration and joy of the moment. And I wanted them to have a piece of the wall as a reminder of this powerful event in history.

Even with all those reasons to go, I didn't act. I lost my sense of urgency. And as a result, I missed a chance to give them a moment we could all share that would have had a long-lasting impact on their lives.

There are times in life when you have to seize an opportunity to make an experience meaningful and to bring the important people in your life into an environment of significance. If you don't anticipate the opportunity, recognize that something is happening, and seize that moment, you can miss those rare occurrences that really matter. I had the time and resources to make the trip to Berlin happen. But I didn't act with intentionality.

Have you ever done that? Have you ever had an idea to do something that could make a difference in the life of another person, yet you let it slip away because you lacked a sense of *urgency*? I have to admit, that's happened too many times in my life. I wish I could seize every opportunity that came my way. I know that's unrealistic, but it's my desire just the same.

In our harried and busy lives, is there ever a *convenient* time to make a difference? Probably not. Is there ever a *right* time? Yes. *It's now—when we see the opportunity!* How do we help ourselves to become more action oriented? We maintain a sense of urgency for making a difference every day.

## Adopting the Right Mindset to Seize Opportunities

I believe every generation gets an opportunity to make a difference, but the people of that generation have to *seize* that opportunity. When Bobby Kennedy was assassinated in 1968, I remember sitting in my

> Every generation gets an opportunity to make a difference, but the people of that generation have to *seize* that opportunity.

living room, reading in the newspaper a quote that was often associated with him and his brother President John F. Kennedy. "There are those that look at things as they are and ask, 'Why?' I dream of things that never were and ask, 'Why not?' "

I was a junior in college in 1968, and this was a defining time for me. There was something about that quote that grabbed me. I understood exactly what Kennedy was saying. And I related to it. I discovered that I was not someone who quit because of obstacles or who would be stopped when others wanted to question *why* something new should be done. I was definitely a possibilities person. I was fearless in my willingness to question what I didn't know—to challenge others with new ways of thinking and doing things. I knew right then I was going to be a person who walked through life asking, "Why not?" I believed in my ability to change things for the better. From that day forward, I tried to seize opportunities and find ways to make things happen.

My journey of significance has been progressive, but it has always been rooted in the desire to act now. I don't wait for tomorrow, next week, next month, next year, or someday when I can get around to taking action. I always focus on *today*. And my sense of urgency has grown as I've gotten older. My significance journey started small but it multiplied as my capability to see bigger developed. It's still developing, and I hope to keep repeating the cycle of growth, with what I do getting bigger and better. But that improvement depends on taking action, on seizing opportunities as they come.

Let me say something about opportunities. They do not multiply because they are *seen*. Many people see opportunities. Opportunities multiply because they are *seized*. And the more people seize opportunities, the more they see them. It becomes a positive cycle. That's why we need to live with a sense of urgency.

> Opportunities do not multiply because they are *seen*....They multiply because they are *seized*.

The saying "you can make a difference at any time, but the best time is now" drives people who possess anticipation and live with intentionality. There is no time like the present. Tomorrow is not guaranteed. Yesterday is too late. Intentional living is a lifestyle, a way of thinking that always says, "There's something more I can do." As poet Ralph Waldo Emerson said, "You cannot do a calling too soon for you never know how soon it will be too late."

## Five Ways to Seize Opportunities

As you step forward into a significant life where you make a difference, you must train yourself to anticipate and seize opportunities. Urgency must become part of your mindset. It must become a lifestyle. If you want to live a great story by making a difference, are willing to start small, have passion, know your *why*, put others first, add value to people from your sweet spot, connect and partner with like-minded and like-valued people, and live with a sense of anticipation, there's only one thing left for you to do to make a difference: seize opportunities.

It will be difficult for me to coach you on the specifics of seizing opportunities, because every person, every situation, and every day is different. But I can show you several places where every person has a chance to seize opportunities to make a difference. You can make a significance impact in the following ways:

### 1. Be the First to Help Someone

I want to ask you to do something. Think about three people who were the first to step up and be there for you at some point in your life when you had a crisis, problem, or dire need. Who helped you when you really needed it?

What was the difficulty you had?

Who was it that stepped forward to help? Write down their names.

What did they do?

OK, now I want you to think really hard for this next question. In that situation, who was the *second* person to help you?

I bet you can't remember, can you? If I offered you a million dollars, you probably couldn't write down that person's name.

Why? The people who most often make the biggest difference are the people who are first to step up and help at a time when it makes a difference.

> The people who most often make the biggest difference are the people who are first to step up and help at a time when it makes a difference.

This has been true in my life. I remember the people who made a difference first: Many years ago Linda Eggers approached me after attending a conference of mine and said if I ever started a company, she would like to help me and be a part of it. She was the first to step up at a time when I needed someone. Linda has now been my executive assistant for more than twenty-five years.

When I came home from the hospital after my heart attack, Charlie Wetzel, my longtime friend and writing collaborator, prepared a wonderful, healthy meal my family and I enjoyed together as I recovered. I'll never forget it because he was the first to celebrate my recovery—and because he happens to be a highly trained chef!

These two people have been a part of my inner circle and in my life for more than two decades. Why? Because they are always anticipating ways to assist me, and when they see an opportunity, they quickly seize the moment. They live with a sense of urgency to make a difference.

When I think of all the books I have written, I smile because of Bud Lunn. He was the first person to offer to help me get a book published when I wanted to write. He was the president of a small publishing company in Kansas City. I can still remember him sharing with me that he thought what I taught others was worthy of being in a book. He said if I wrote the book, he would publish it for me free of charge.

While I was considering his proposal, Les Parrott was the first to explain to me why I should write my first book. He told me I would probably never make any money doing it, but I could help people. To this day that is still my motivation for writing. My favorite days of all time are the days my books hit bookstores.

Why?

There's nothing better than the thrill I get looking at that book, holding it in my hands, knowing it will help people. I can tell you every place I was on the day I saw the first copy of one of my books and held it in my hands for the first time.

I remember the first person who gave money to EQUIP. It was Gerald Brooks, a pastor friend of mine in Texas, who had watched me train leaders for years. I was in a small room where I used to pray and work at Skyline Church when Dottie, my assistant at the time, came running up with an envelope in her hand.

"Pastor! Look at this!" she said, waving a white envelope like it was the American flag.

It was a check for $10,000 along with a short note from Gerald that said, "I know you have a heart to train leaders. I wanted to be the first to encourage you to go out and do it. Put this toward training leaders."

Gerald's belief in me meant everything. When he stepped forward and wrote that first check, he inspired me to go out and raise millions of dollars, and he opened the door for me to train hundreds of thousands of leaders. He was the one who leveraged all of that significance because he was the first to say, "I believe in you, John."

When I think about all these people who stepped

up first in my life at a time when it made a difference, I realize...

- They set themselves apart from all of the others.
- They will always have a special place in my heart.
- They planted the first seeds of success in my life.
- Their seeds compounded into a bountiful harvest of significant living!

When you receive the kind of support and belief that I have, there is tremendous motivation and desire to provide that type of inspiration to other people, too. Every morning that I am booked to speak to a group I wake up with great anticipation because I believe I am going to make a difference in people's lives that day.

It never fails to happen to me: my expectation, eagerness, and anticipation are off the charts. By the time I get to the venue, I am almost kid-like with excitement. As I am teaching, I am filled with great joy because I know, without a doubt, I am giving the group something that will work and has the potential to transform their lives. I understand the impact the information I am handing over can have if they take action. I know what's possible if they seize the opportunity.

Are you on the lookout for opportunities where you can be the first to help people? The first to encourage them? The first to open doors that they cannot open on their own? Do you have a sense of urgency? Look around. Maybe you can be the first to encourage a member of your family. Maybe you can help someone you're ahead of at work to solve a problem, acquire a skill, or benefit from your experience. Maybe you can come to the aid of a neighbor or a stranger. The opportunities are there. You just need to open your eyes, recognize them, and *seize* them.

## 2. Take a Risk When the Potential for Significance Is High

In 2010, my friend Scott Fay, who owns a landscaping company, introduced me to his friend Paul Martinelli. They had the idea to partner with me to create a coaching company that could certify and train people to become coaches, teachers, and speakers according to my values and using some of my materials. They wanted to call it the John Maxwell Team.

I was sixty-three years old then, and I wasn't sure whether I wanted to do it. I was at a crossroads at that time. I had just created the John Maxwell Company, and I could sense that I was entering a season of heightened opportunities for significance. But I had two conflicting emotions about starting a coaching company. On the one hand, I was excited and intrigued. It was a great opportunity. What would happen if I offered my name and reputation to people who really wanted to make a difference in the lives of others? How many people would be interested in being trained? When they became trained, how many people would they be able to add value to? Would this endeavor help launch them into a journey of significance? How many difference makers would want to be a part of this movement? How long would it take to begin noticeably enlarging our significance circle? Each question raised the level of my anticipation. What a great opportunity!

But I also had doubts, so I began asking other questions. Could my principles of life and leadership be faithfully passed on to others so that they would begin to multiply? Could we train people to be world-class coaches? What kind of risk would I be taking if I lent my name to people we recruited whom I didn't really know? What if a coach we certified did something crazy or negative? What if one of them messed up? What would that do the reputation I'd worked forty years to build? Would it negatively impact my ability to add value to others? Would it hurt the members of my team who had worked hard to build my other organizations and my brand?

This was the area where I had my greatest hesitancy—the risk to the other companies I'd built, and the people who worked for them. I had to work through this concern before I could move forward. I had to come to peace with the idea that there would eventually be people representing the John Maxwell Team who would mess up. But if you're going to live significantly, you can't take yourself so seriously that you hesitate because you're worried about what other people might think or do. If that worries you too much, you stop yourself from accomplishing greater things.

I couldn't be tied to the opinions of others. When you give yourself to others, there is a sense of vulnerability. I can control my own little world, but the moment I try to move outside of it to do something of significance, there are some things that are not in my control. I had to accept that reality and its risks, and then remind myself that significance yields a greater return any time I can do something more for others than I can do for myself.

I knew I wanted to have my legacy continue on after I was gone. Paul knew how to build a great coaching company. And Scott helped to bring us together. So I made the decision to move forward and create the John Maxwell Team. Today Paul and Scott do a fantastic job of leading that team, and we have more than seven thousand certified coaches in more than one hundred countries.

The main reason I took this step was that the timing was right for me to start building my legacy, because my age and reputation had gotten to a place where I felt I could justify it. And I felt a sense of urgency. If I had tried to start a coaching company even ten years earlier, I could not have justified it because I didn't have the credibility or experience. Back then even my own mother wouldn't have joined! But now I felt I had something to give. And I could actually give it because I would be able to partner with the right people who could help me build this kind of organization. At the time, not everyone in my inner circle thought it was a good idea. It took them time to come on board, but now they see the value it brings to so many people.

What opportunities to make a difference do you see that you know hold risks? How do you know when the risk is worth the effort? How do you know the timing is right? These are tough questions. You can do what I often do and make a list of the pros and cons and weigh them against one another. You can do a risk analysis where you chart the probability against the consequences. If you're a person of faith, you can pray.

The process is different for everybody. But let me say this: Don't ever dismiss an opportunity just because it has risks—because everything has risks. You could fear risk so much that you decide never to leave the safety of your home... yet you could still die if a tree fell on your bedroom while you slept or your house caught fire. If you're going to have a bias in a direction, have a bias toward action. In the end, people most often regret the chances they *failed* to take, not the chances they took that failed.

> People most often regret the chances they *failed* to take, not the chances they took that failed.

## 3. Do What You Know Is Right, Even with No Promise of Return

We often tend to judge opportunities by the potential return. There's nothing wrong with that. In fact, I encourage you to be strategic in your thinking. However, there are also times when we are faced with opportunities to do things that we know are right, even if we don't know where they will lead or what will result.

I want to encourage you to follow through and

seize these kinds of opportunities, because the return on giving is always higher than what we give. I'm still surprised by the impact a simple act can have on someone, but I am never surprised by the outcome of intentional living.

Whenever I write a book or record a CD, I believe it will help someone. I don't always know who, when, or where, but I know without a doubt that it will have a significant impact, and that's what keeps me motivated to keep seizing these kinds of opportunities.

A few years ago I received a handwritten note from a man who had been terribly lost and confused. He felt the need to share his story with me, as the outcome was so powerful and unexpected for him. He wrote,

> *Mr. Maxwell,*
>
> *I want to thank you for the value you have added to my life, but the word "value" just doesn't seem to be a worthy word for what you have done for me.*
>
> *I would like to briefly explain my story and how you have impacted my life. My parents tried unsuccessfully for thirteen years to have a child, decided to adopt, and found me. Within eighteen months my mom was pregnant with my little brother. Growing up in south Georgia, I did well*

*in school until I reached thirteen years old. I then disobeyed my parents and went against God for the first time in a way I felt was unforgivable with a girl I knew from our neighborhood. This choice sent me into a pattern of rebellion and mistrust. At seventeen years old, I tried drugs for the first time and became addicted and hopeless.*

*By twenty-one I was married to an amazing girl who had no idea of my addiction. During this time I had two businesses and debt in excess of $1.5 million without anything to show for it, and our checking account was $99,000 overdrawn. Within two years I was going through a divorce with my wife, who I had driven away. She left me for one of my employees and my life was destroyed.*

*I decided to take my life. I went to the attic of my house to hang myself, and there in a dusty old attic, on a plywood floor, for the first time in my life I experienced God's unconditional love! I met Jesus.*

*I was given one of your CDs by one of your team members and as I began to listen to it over and over (more than thirty times), your words were, and continue to be, used by God to give me hope and build a bridge for me to believe God can and will work in my life.*

*Your words took me from the attic, wanting to kill myself, to reconciling with my wife (we've been together fifteen years now), believing God to not declare bankruptcy, [and] repenting my way out of incredible debt. Now we own five companies, pastor an incredible group of leaders, run two nonprofits, and have the opportunity to influence thousands of people by investing what was given to me by you into the lives of others.*

Thank you is not ENOUGH, but it's a start!

*What can you say when someone saves your life and then helps you build a new one that is greater than you could dream of?*

*God's kindness and your willingness to give your life away to others makes this kind of impact possible! I owe you my life in so many ways! I commit to allowing God to continually give away to others the wisdom you have given me. I appreciate you SO much. Thank you.*

This gentleman credits me with saving his life, but I don't see it that way. All I did was record a CD because it was in line with my *why* and I knew it would help someone, somewhere, sometime. I may not know *when* that is going to happen, but I know it *will* happen. And that's why I do it.

And that's why you should perform intentional acts of significance. If you maintain a sense of urgency and obey your instinct to do the right thing, especially when it plays to your strengths, it may have a greater impact than you would ever dream. I embrace the words of the apostle Paul, who advised, "So let's not allow ourselves to get fatigued doing good. At the right time we will harvest a good crop if we don't give up, or quit. Right now, therefore, every time we get the chance, let us work for the benefit of all."[29] Even if you aren't a person of faith, you can embrace these words because you probably instinctively know that you reap what you sow.

## 4. Give to Your Peers at a Time When It Makes a Difference

I had the opportunity to connect with Condoleezza Rice a few years ago, and I found out she was teaching freshmen at Stanford University. I was curious about what motivated her to return to teaching after her career in Washington was done. After all, she had been to the highest peak, sitting in the most influential meetings in the world with incredible people, listening and participating in the most intense and purposeful discussions. She had been a part of the world's most powerful think tanks. And yet, now, she was back in the classroom. I wanted to know if this was something she planned to do for a year or two and then move on, or if she was looking at a longer-term commitment. Condoleezza explained that her decision to teach was deliberate and full of intention:

> The classroom is the molder of the opinion of the lives of people. I came back because if I can change a nineteen-year-old's life, that is much more significant than what I was doing because I get them on the front end.

I loved her answer and the notion of impacting people on the front end of their lives, especially young people who have great potential and just need someone, like a teacher, a coach, or a boss, to come along and believe in them.

I like to think of myself as a lid-lifter in people's lives. I love to find people I believe in and in whom I see great potential, and come into their lives through what I teach or through words of encouragement to follow their dreams of significance. Though I have lifted the lid on many in the pastorate, one of the most significant people I've been able to serve is Bill Hybels, the founding and senior pastor of Willow Creek Community Church in South Barrington, Illinois. Today, his church is one of the largest in North America and is considered one of the most influential in the world.

Back in 1995 I was teaching leadership seminars,

and I invited Bill to join me. He was fantastic, and his leadership messages were off the charts. Though Bill is a tremendous communicator and leader, he had not done much teaching on leadership beyond his own staff. I told him that he needed to teach leadership to a broader audience, because I knew it would help people. In response to one particular message, I told Bill, "You need to teach this two hundred times."

Soon afterward, Bill started the Global Leadership Summit, an annual training event for church, ministry, and other leaders to sharpen their skills. The Global Leadership Summit exists to transform Christian leaders around the world with an injection of vision, skill development, and inspiration for the sake of the local church. The Summit telecasts live from the campus of Willow Creek Community Church near Chicago, reaching more than 185 host sites across the United States. Guests that Bill's had onstage have included leaders and thinkers such as Bill Clinton, Jack Welch, Jim Collins, and Bono.

As I was writing this book, Bill hosted his twentieth Leadership Summit. I received an e-mail from him that made me smile. It read,

*Dear John,*
*Just a quick thank you. We just had our twentieth summit here in North America, God rocked it!*

*95,000 people. 110,000 more outside the United States. Had you not challenged me to start teaching leadership, I doubt this would have happened.*

*Bill*

Bill wasn't looking for my help. He was already doing great things. He just needed someone to come along and point out a new opportunity for adding value to people different from what he was already doing. I knew he could be a difference maker by helping people in the field of leadership. I saw he had the power to change people's lives. He just needed someone to encourage him to do it, which I was glad to do.

I have benefitted from the help of other leaders even more than I've helped others. Many people have added value to me. For example, when I had my heart attack, my friend Jack Hayford, who is an author and a pastor, called me and said he'd handle any and all requests for speaking engagements for the next six months for me so I could recover, focus on my health, and get stronger. He stepped in at a time that really mattered to me. He understood that I would have a hard time saying no to the invitations, so he offered to say yes for me and take my place. What a great friendship and blessing in my life that allowed me to recover.

How can you come alongside a peer and help him or her? What opportunities are presenting themselves right now? Not someday. Not when it's more convenient. Right now. Who could you give a leg up? I guarantee there's somebody in your life who could use your help and who would be forever grateful.

## 5. Plant the Seeds of Intentionality in Children

One of the most important things we can do is pass along to the next generation what we've learned. I do that every day as I train leaders, develop my team, and speak to people on personal growth. But the place where it's most important to me is close to home. Margaret and I planted the seeds of our values in our children, and now we are doing it with our grandchildren. And one of the most important seeds we plant is intentionality.

When we are young, the books our parents read to us have the power to imprint values upon us and encourage us, even at the youngest age. Early reading is how many children learn life's basics, including colors, numbers, letters, and stories. So much of the information that we store in our brains as we grow older and mature is put there in our early years.

I love the books of Dr. Seuss. He was very clever in placing intentional messages of significance within his books, and those seeds have been planted in millions of children at an early age. His writing has been taught in classrooms for years because of the simple yet poignant nature of his messages. If we shared Dr. Seuss's message with every child, it would have the power to impact and change the world.

Here's what I mean. Look at lines such as these:

"Unless someone like you cares a whole awful lot, nothing is going to get better. It's not."[30]

"You have brains in your head. You have feet in your shoes. You can steer yourself in any direction you choose."[31]

"You're off to great places! Today is your day! Your mountain is waiting! So get on your way!"[32]

Though each of these lines comes within the context of a story, they communicate important life lessons that can never be given too early to kids. The sooner they understand the value of living with intentionality, the more quickly they can start living lives of significance. What we teach our children to love and appreciate is far more important than what we teach them to know.

> What we teach our children to love and appreciate is far more important than what we teach them to know.

As a result of my parents being so intentional with me, I became an extremely intentional parent with my own children. Thankfully, Margaret and I saw eye to eye on this need in our child-rearing years, and our kids reaped the benefits of our actions.

Margaret intentionally took the kids to school every morning. She never let them take the bus because she wanted the last words they would hear before they went off to class each day to be positive ones from her. She was also purposely at home when they were done with classes and their extracurricular activities. Margaret was always making sure they had a comfortable place to sit and tell her about their day. Not everyone can do that, but if you could, why wouldn't you?

Today, my grandchildren also reap the benefits of the intentionality my parents instilled in me as a child, though their methods of retaining the lessons we teach tend to be a bit more high tech than mine were. My granddaughter Maddie keeps a running list of principles either her dad (my son-in-law, Steve) or I teach her. She also records poignant lines she reads from some of my books. She keeps all these things in her iPhone. Every time she comes across a new quote, she adds it to her "Daddy/Papa List."

Recently I asked her to share with me some of the things she has captured. Here are a few of them:

- Attitude is a choice.
- Maturity is seeing things from another person's point of view and being flexible.
- Always plan ahead. You're either prepared or repaired.
- You are what you do every day.
- Failure is inevitable, but learning is optional.

Having a list like this helps Maddie value herself and build her self-esteem. Sometimes she and I will talk about one of the quotes on her list so that I can reinforce that principle or lesson. I prefer talking to her in person whenever possible, though as a teenager, she likes to text. I don't want to lose the opportunity to strengthen her intentionality, so I will send her reminders and follow up with her to make sure we are always in touch. It's a really great way for me to be connected to my granddaughter, something I appreciate and I know she does, too.

Margaret and I are even intentional at Christmas. Our gift to our children and grandchildren every year is a trip. We want to have wonderful experiences together while we can. During these trips each member of our family knows that I will ask them two questions: "What did you love, and what did you learn?"

I asked this when my children were young, and I still ask it. Why? Because our best teacher isn't experience. It's evaluated experience. Answering those questions prompts them to evaluate what they've experienced. We are intentional in making sure that each experience becomes a lesson that can be learned and understood for their personal development.

Our family tradition at Christmas is to give the first gift to Jesus since it is his birthday. All year long, our grandchildren put aside money in their Jesus bank. Then on Christmas Eve, they give the first gift to the charity of their choice.

This Christmas season I was playing golf with Tom Mullins, the president of EQUIP, when he said, "John, this week your grandchildren, Hannah, John, and James, brought their birthday gift for Jesus to me and wanted the money to go to EQUIP." As the founder of EQUIP and their papa, I was so proud of them! It didn't improve my golf game, but it did make me grateful. Their gift was the result of their parents' being intentional with them.

Don't miss your opportunity to pour intentionality into the lives of your children or grandchildren. It is never too early to start. If you can create a significance mindset in them when they are young, you don't have to try to create it later in life. They won't have to break old habits or create new ones to start living a life that matters. They will already have those habits.

Having the courage and responsibility to instill intentionality in our children can change the way they live. The possibilities are boundless and the timing critical. You have to possess a sense of urgency in this area because the time we have with our children and grandchildren is really very short.

My dream is to raise up a generation of intentional people. It may not be this generation, or even the next one. But if the next generation has the seeds planted early on and then believes in the power of intentionality, imagine the impact they could have on the world they live in.

## Making a Difference Every Day

My greatest hope is that people everywhere will become intentional in seizing opportunities to make a difference and to transform their families, businesses, neighborhoods, communities, cities, and countries. I believe that when we follow the path of wanting to make a difference, by doing something that makes a difference, with people who make a difference, at a time that makes a difference, we can change the world and make it a better place.

Author and speaker Jim Collins says, "Transformation can only happen if you have transformational leaders." Jim has studied transformational leadership culture more than anyone else has, so I believe he's right. That's why I'm working so hard right now to help others live intentionally and influence others for positive change.

Recently I met a transformational leader whose story inspires me to keep trying to make a difference, and I believe his story will also inspire you. His name is Jeff Williams. He is an independent business owner who is highly intentional and is making a difference every day.

Jeff's journey to significance began when he was only eight years old. He grew up in a family of very modest means. They didn't have much. They got by, but there were no extras. Jeff says that on the rare occasion that they went to McDonald's, his parents would buy him a burger, but he'd never get the fries or a drink. That's how tight things were at home for him growing up.

One day a salesman in a suit showed up at Jeff's house with a sample case full of books called *Uncle Arthur's Bedtime Stories.* Jeff remembers peeking around the edge of the dining room doorway hearing the salesman's pitch to his parents in their living room. "These books are so well made," the salesman said, "a child can make a mess with peanut butter and jam, and it will wipe right off."

*That's what I eat for lunch!* Jeff thought as he listened.

Jeff was shocked when his parents splurged and bought a set of the books.

It was a life-changing opportunity.

Every night Jeff's mom or dad would read him one of the stories. Jeff loved them so much, he would sometimes stay up late and read ahead.

One night Jeff's parents read a story that would change his life. To this day he remembers it vividly. It was called "Wilfred's Secret." It was the story of a boy and his sister who decided to create what they called "The Surprise Package Company," where they secretly left gifts for sick kids laid up in bed or anonymously gave food to shut-in old ladies.

The story inspired Jeff right down to his soul. "Something just ignited on the inside of me," says Jeff. "Doing that would be so cool, to be a blessing to other people and surprise people. And for me the great thrill was watching them discover the surprise without their knowing I was there. And to see the delight in their eyes."

So Jeff enlisted the aid of his sister, and they started doing what the brother and sister in the story did. They gave away some of their toys and made crafts, which they gave to people anonymously. "That was the seed of generosity that God has gifted me with," says Jeff.

Jeff's life turned upside down just a few years after that, and his family life turned, in Jeff's words, "crazy." But the desire to make a difference was already inside of him.

Flash forward more than a decade, and Jeff, though young, was married and had four children. He worked in the restaurant business and then in direct marketing. They didn't have much, but they were always givers.

Jeff remembers a young couple who had worked with them in direct marketing, but had then left the business. They were struggling. Jeff and his family bought a bunch of groceries for them. He and the kids put the groceries on their doorstep, then hid in bushes around the corner as a stranger they recruited rang the couple's doorbell. Secretly watching their reaction and knowing they had made a difference made him and his kids feel good.

Jeff experienced modest success in direct marketing, but the thing that had most inspired him was the realization that if he made a lot of money, he could give a lot away. And that became his dream. Soon, he started his own company. After years of hard work, the company began to be successful.

By the time I met Jeff, he was already making a difference in the lives of others. When I traveled to Guatemala in 2013 to teach values in roundtables, he traveled with us. There he met a man named Carlos who was taking care of orphans and saving malnourished children from starvation. Jeff recognized that Carlos was a like-valued person, and they began partnering together to make a difference. Jeff has funded the building of a small village for orphans with Carlos in Guatemala. And every month Jeff pays to send some of his employees and their families to Guatemala to serve there.

Jeff has also along come alongside me, and we are partnering together to make a difference. Jeff has helped me and EQUIP to develop technology to start a transformational effort in the seven streams of influence: arts, entertainment, sports, and culture; business; education; family; faith; government; and media.

One of the things I love most about Jeff is that he is just as intentional and entrepreneurial about making a difference as he is about developing his business. He lives each day with a strong sense of urgency for significance. And the gains he makes in the marketplace are being put to greater use to serve others.

"The other day I came up with this business idea," said Jeff, "and I got so excited because immediately I thought, *Wow, this is going to be successful. It's going to make my company more successful, and now I can give away extra money next October. Where do I want to give that?*"

What Jeff is living is also being passed on to his children. Recently he learned that when his daughter

Deanna was twelve, she quietly and secretly saved her allowance and other money to sponsor seven under-privileged children at a summer horse camp that Jeff and his family worked with. At $225 per child, that means Deanna had given over $1,500!

Always intentional, Jeff is actively looking for ways to make a difference on a continual basis. And I love his big-picture goal the most. "I hope one day to use my story to challenge a thousand other businesspeople to do the same thing: to pick a project, get involved, fund it, and get their staff involved, too." Now that's significance. If everybody thought like Jeff and had his sense of urgency, the world would change in no time.

When you live intentionally, you wake up anticipating that you will change people's lives every day. You look for opportunities everywhere, and when you see one that taps into your *why* and adds value from your sweet spot, you seize it. Jeff does that every day. So do I. *So can you!* All you have to do is possess a sense of urgency and seize the moment. It doesn't have to be big. It doesn't have to be

> Once you taste significance, success will never satisfy you again.

earth-shattering. It just needs to be for others. If we can do it, so can you. You can taste significance, and once you taste significance, success will never satisfy you again.

# Intentional Application:
# Be Urgent about Seizing Significance Opportunities

## Become an Entrepreneur for Significance

I love spending time with business entrepreneurs. I love their creativity, their work ethic, their sense of urgency, and their willingness to risk. But as much as I enjoy spending time with them, I love being with significance entrepreneurs even more. These are people who...

- See things that unintentional people do not see.
- Believe things that unintentional people do not believe.
- Feel things that unintentional people do not feel.
- Say things that unintentional people do not say.
- Do things that unintentional people do not do.

Take a look at each of those five phrases and write about each of them. What opportunities do you see that others don't? What do you believe and feel about them? What are you willing to say that others are afraid to say about them? What are you willing to do? Put together all of those ideas to write a manifesto of intentional significance that you can live by.

## Be More Intentional Helping Children

I believe it is impossible to be too intentional in helping children. If you're a parent or grandparent, start with the children in your family. If they're young enough, read to them. If I could do only one thing to help the children of the world, it would be to teach them to read well. A person who can read can learn to do anything else.

Become intentional about everything you do with your children. Talk to them continually to encourage them. Teach them in any way you can, including on vacations. Model good values. Help them to reach their potential.

If you don't have children of your own, help a younger sibling. Spend time with a niece or nephew. Volunteer at a school. Offer to mentor a young person. Find a way to add value to people of the next generation, especially from your sweet spot. An investment in them is an investment in significance.

## Who Needs Help?

Who among your peers could use a hand? See that as an opportunity to add value and seize it as an avenue into significant living. If you give with no expectation of return, you can make a difference and live a life that matters.

# EPILOGUE

## Tell Others Your Story

I'm currently sixty-eight years old. People sometimes ask me why I don't slow down. "Why are you pressing?" they ask. Because my age tells me that my time is limited. I'm reminded of the words of King David of ancient Israel, who wrote, "Teach me O Lord about the end of my life. Teach me about the number of my days I have left so I may know how temporary my life is."[33]

I know my time is limited. I want my life to matter. I want to be significant. I know that if I want to make a difference, I need to live with intentionality and a sense of urgency.

If I want to make a difference, I need to do it *now*.

What about you? Do you have a sense of urgency for making a difference? You may be younger than I am and feel you have plenty of time left.

Do you?

If you start now—today—then the answer is yes. You still have time to do something significant. Why? Because significance is not a *destination* thing—it's a *daily* thing. As my mentor John Wooden used to say, "Make every day your masterpiece." Significance is not about someday; it's about today. You can make a difference anytime—but the best time is *now*.

> Significance is not a *destination* thing— it's a *daily* thing.

## A Life with No Regrets

I once asked Coach John Wooden if he had any regrets about decisions he had made throughout his life.

"I have none," he said.

His answer shocked me.

*"None?"* I asked.

"I made every decision with a pure heart, the right heart. If you asked me if all of my decisions were good, I'd tell you they weren't. But you didn't ask me that. You asked if I regret any."

I looked at him with great wonder and admiration. Surely, I have not known many people throughout my life who could have given me this same answer with such confidence. In fact, at the time he said it, I could not think of any!

"You see, John, I did the very best that I could at that time to make each decision. Is there anything else you can expect from yourself?"

That conversation had a profound impact on me. I wish I had made every decision with good motives, but I can't say with integrity that I always have. I've done more than my share of dumb things. I've made mistakes. I've had wrong motives. You know that because I've told you a lot of my story. I didn't tell it because I want you to do things my way or be like me. I'm not trying to hold myself up as a model. In fact, I wish I could have figured out a way to teach you about intentional living and significance *without* having to tell my story. But this is the only way I know how to do it. Still, I don't want to go through life with regret—not for any reason. Even when I have made mistakes along the way, I've used those experiences to learn and grow. They've made me stronger, smarter, and more thoughtful along the way. I want you to learn from my mistakes, just as I have. Maybe I can save you a few steps.

You see, we all go through life doing the best we can. We can't legitimately offer more than we know. We can't perform at a higher level than our experiences have taught us to or come to a greater place than our expertise has brought us to. However, once you have opened yourself up to something new—to the possibility of what can be—it's hard to ignore the potential we see. At least, it always has been for me.

You can try, but ultimately, you really can't unlearn what you know. Sure, you can choose not to practice it. You can stash it away, push it to the back of your memory bank, and pretend it doesn't exist. But once the information has traveled into the portals of your mind, it's there, it's ready, and it's calling for action. What you do with that information is up to you. Whether you practice the principle you know to be true is simply a choice. And it's yours alone to make.

## What Will Your Decision Be?

Now you know how to live a life that matters. You know what it means to be intentional. So I want to ask you a series of questions. See how many you can honestly answer yes to:

- ☐ Are you choosing to live a story of significance?
- ☐ Are you choosing to live with intentionality, not just good intentions?

- [ ] Are you willing to start small but believe big to make a difference?
- [ ] Are you actively searching for your *why* so that you can make a difference?
- [ ] Have you put other people first to make a difference?
- [ ] Are you trying to add value to others from your sweet spot to make a difference?
- [ ] Are you connecting with like-minded people who make a difference?
- [ ] Are you trying to partner with like-valued people to make a difference?
- [ ] Are you living with a sense of anticipation for making a difference?
- [ ] Are you seizing opportunities and taking action to make a difference?

If you answered yes to all of these questions—or if you are willing to answer yes and take action *now*—then you have crossed over into the significant life. You will make a difference. Your life will matter. And you will start to change the world. You've made the decision. Now you just need to manage that decision every day of your life. You just need to keep living intentionally and take action in some small way every day.

## What's Your Story?

If you have crossed over, I want to hear about it. I want to know your story of significance. I want you to tell me and others about how you seized an opportunity to make a difference and took action. It can be small or big. It can be your first or your best. It can be a story of heart or hope, humor or help. It can be a paragraph, a poem, a series of photos, or a video. The only important thing is that it's *your* story.

I've even created a place for you to tell it. It's a website called **MyIntentionalLivingStory.com**. Go there and tell the world how you're making a difference. My dream is to help one million people become intentional, start making a difference, and tell their stories. I want you to be a part of that.

Years ago, I read a poem by Lawrence Tribble that has always stayed with me. It says,

> *One man awake, awakens another.*
> *The second awakens his next door brother.*
> *The three awake can rouse a town*
> *By turning the whole place upside down.*
> *The many awake can cause such a fuss*
> *It finally awakens the rest of us.*
> *One man up with dawn in his eyes*
> *Surely then multiplies.*[34]

If you join me in my dream of making a difference, together maybe we can start a movement—a movement toward a world of intentional living where people think of others before themselves, where adding value to others is a priority, where financial gain is second to future potential, and where people's self-worth is strengthened by acts of significance every day.

If we each live a life that truly matters, we can change the world. Until then, I want to leave you with these words from a Franciscan blessing:

*May God bless you with discomfort,*
*At easy answers, half-truths,*
*And superficial relationships*
*So that you may live*
*Deep within your heart.*

*May God bless you with anger*
*At injustice, oppression,*
*And exploitation of people,*
*So that you may work for*
*Justice, freedom, and peace.*

*May God bless you with tears,*
*To shed for those who suffer pain,*
*Rejection, hunger, and war,*

*So that you may reach out your hand*
*To comfort them and*
*To turn their pain to joy*

*And may God bless you*
*With enough foolishness*
*To believe that you can*
*Make a difference in the world,*
*So that you can do*
*What others claim cannot be done*
*To bring justice and kindness*
*To all our children and the poor.*
*Amen.*[35]

# Notes

1. Donald Miller, *A Million Miles in a Thousand Years: What I Learned While Editing My Life* (Nashville: Thomas Nelson, 2009), 59–60.
2. Ibid., 86.
3. Victor Goertzel and Mildred Goertzel, *Cradles of Eminence* (Boston: Little, Brown, 1978).
4. Miller, *A Million Miles*, 236–237.
5. Alexandra Sifferlin, "Here's How the ALS Ice Bucket Challenge Actually Started," *Time*, August 18, 2014, http://time.com/3136507/als-ice-bucket-challenge -started/, accessed January 29, 2015.
6. Proverbs 18:21, MSG.
7. NIV.
8. Philippians 4:13, NKJV.
9. MSG.
10. Dolly Parton, "Dolly's Dreams," Guideposts, http://www .guideposts.org/inspiration/inspirational-stories/dollys -dreams, accessed December 8, 2014.
11. Jack Canfield and Mark Victor Hansen, *Chicken Soup for the Soul* (Deerfield Beach, FL: Health Communications, 1993), 18–20.
12. Kevin Hall, *Aspire: Discovering Your Purpose through the Power of Words* (New York: William Morrow, 2010), 58.

13. Luke 22:27, MSG.
14. Charles Royden, "Sermon preached by Reverend Charles Royden," http://www.thisischurch.com/christian_teaching/sermon/lordsprayer.htm, accessed February 16, 2015.
15. Cahal Milmo, "Mohamed El-Erian Reveals Daughter's Talk Led to PIMCO Exit," *The Independent*, September 24, 2014, http://www.independent.co.uk/news/business/us-financier-quits-2trn-investment-fund-after-his-daughter-writes-list-showing-22-life-landmarks-hed-missed-9754002.html?origin=internalSearch, accessed February 17, 2015.
16. Mohamel El-Erian, "Father and Daughter Reunion," *Worth*, http://www.worth.com/index.php/component/content/article/4-live/6722-father-and-daughter-reunion, accessed February 17, 2015.
17. Phyllis McCormack, "Crabbit Old Woman," originally appeared in *Nursing Mirror*, December 1972.
18. Kate Kellaway, "Giles Duley: 'My friends love the idea of me being half man, half camera,'" *The Observer*, October 29, 2011, http://www.theguardian.com/artanddesign/2011/oct/30/giles-duley-war-photography-afghanistan?CMP=email, accessed March 9, 2015.
19. "Becoming the Story: Giles Duley at TEDxObserver," TED Talk, http://www.ted.com/talks/giles_duley_when_a_reporter_becomes_the_story, accessed March 9, 2015.
20. Kellaway, "Giles Duley."
21. "This Veteran Has Returned More than 100 Lost or Stolen Purple Heart Medals to Families," *The Huffington Post*, August 8, 2014, http://www.huffingtonpost.com/2014/08/08/zachariah-fike-purple-hearts-reunited_n_5662751.html, accessed February 26, 2015.

22. Robert Kiener, "The Hearts of Soldiers," *Reader's Digest*, March 2015, 84–85.

23. "This Veteran."

24. Craig Stanley, "Captain's Mission: Reunite Purple Heart Medals with Recipients' Families," NBCNews, August 18, 2012, http://dailynightly.nbcnews.com/_news/2012/08/18/13355743-captains-mission-reunite-purple-heart-medals-with-recipients-families?lite, accessed February 26, 2015.

25. "How to Participate," Super Service Challenge [website], http://www.superservicechallenge.com/how-to-participate/?1425317776420, accessed March 2, 2015.

26. "Super Service Challenge History," Super Service Challenge [website], http://www.superservicechallenge.com/about-us/?1418399371737, accessed December 12, 2014.

27. Jason Falconer, "Teen's Inexpensive 3D-Printed Prosthetic Could Aid Amputees in the Third World," *Gizmag*, August 13, 2013, http://www.gizmag.com/easton-lachappelle-3d-printed-prosthetic/28685/, accessed March 4, 2015.

28. Dominique Mosbergen, "At 14, He Vowed to Invent an Affordable Limb. 5 Years Later, He's Succeeded," *The Huffington Post*, January 27, 2015, http://www.huffingtonpost.com/2015/01/27/easton-lachappelle-prosthetic-robotic-arm-hand_n_6556458.html, accessed March 4, 2015.

29. Galatians 6:9–10, MSG.

30. Dr. Seuss, *The Lorax* (New York: Random House, 1971).

31. Dr. Seuss, *Oh, the Places You'll Go!* (New York: Random House, 1960).

32. Ibid.

33. Psalm 39:4, GW.

34. Lawrence Tribble, "Awaken," circa 1780s, Push Back Now [website], http://pushbacknow.net/2011/10/31/awaken-a -1700s-poem-by-lawrence-tribble/comment-page-1/, accessed December 13, 2014.

35. "A Franciscan Blessing," Franciscans Na Proinnsiasaigh Irish Franciscans OFM [website], http://www.franciscans .ie/news/83-news-scroller/485-a-franciscan-blessing, accessed December 13, 2014.

# Look for John C. Maxwell's other bestselling books

# John C. Maxwell's Bestselling Successful People Series
## Perfect compact reads for today's
## fast-paced world

MAKE
TODAY
COUNT

HOW
SUCCESSFUL
PEOPLE
THINK

HOW
SUCCESSFUL
PEOPLE
LEAD

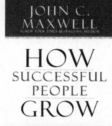

HOW
SUCCESSFUL
PEOPLE
GROW

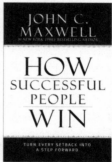
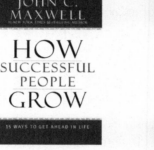

HOW
SUCCESSFUL
PEOPLE
WIN

## And in summer 2016 look for

LEADERSHIP
ANSWERS
TO YOUR
TOUGHEST
QUESTIONS

Also available in Spanish and from ⬡ hachette AUDIO and ⬡ hachette DIGITAL

Available from Center Street wherever books are sold.

CENTER
STREET

Stop looking for a life that matters—*start living it!*

# The 7 DAY Experiment

Do you know what the most popular day of the week is for most people?

**Tomorrow.**

Tomorrow I'll start exercising. Tomorrow I'll start reading that book. Tomorrow I'll clean the house. Tomorrow, tomorrow, tomorrow.

The problem? **Today** is the only day you can *do* anything.

That's why John Maxwell created the new **7-Day Experiment** to help you exchange those tomorrows for todays.

All it takes is 7 days to start transforming your life. It is never too late to live a life that matters. All you need is the courage to start with small actions but believe big. John will guide the way.

Start *your* journey toward intentional living and significance.

To begin your FREE 7-day journey visit

**7DayExperiment.com**.

Better yet, invite a friend and do it together.